TANYA MAGNUS

Editor-Amy Van Vleck & Brenda Smith

Editorial Advisor-Brenda Smith

Text Formatting- Sally Jones

Cover Design-Medea Peabody

Author Photo-Scott Dalrymple srichardsphotography.com

Prayer Warriors-Lynne Freauf, Pat Walters, Karin Jones, Brenda Smith, Karen King, Melissa Randolph, Sally Jones

All Scripture references taken from the New International Version (NIV) @1983 unless otherwise noted.

Published by Choose To Soar Ministries, www.choosetosoar.net

First revision 2010

Table of Contents

Acknowledgments

Introduction

Chapter

Acknowledgments

I don't even know where to start except to say the writing of this project has been one of the hardest and yet most joyful things I have ever done. And I couldn't have done it without the help of so many. I was truly blessed by being surrounded by a team of wonderful friends whose passion is to glorify our Lord.

My gratitude runs deep for those who played such a major part in this project. To Sally Jones, my friend and faithful assistant who is always willing to do anything I need, whether it means making power point slides, copies, learning new software or even helping my child with her homework. Thank you for countless hours you put into this project, especially at crunch time. What a servant's heart you have. I don't know how to thank you Sally, but know I thank God for you daily! To my dear wise friend, Brenda Smith, your coaching throughout the writing process has been invaluable to me. Your words of encouragement always give me great strength and wind beneath my wings. Thank you a thousand times over.

Of course none of this could have been possible without the amazing prayers of my friends who are true Prayer Warriors. A great big thank you goes to Lynne Freauf, for the daily texting of prayers and encouragement, for being such a great friend. Your endless support and love has filled me up many times. I am ready to go to another game, sponge finger and all. Thank you Pat Walters for your prayers but mainly for being one of my bestest friends ever. You are family, sort of like a big sister (notice I didn't say older sister). I miss playing golf with you. To Karin Jones, your emails of encouragement and prayers have blessed me. Every time I see you, your face shines with eagerness to pray and learn more about our Lord, this inspires me so. Thank you my friend. To Karen King, what a constant support you have been for me. Your prayers, your thoughtful words, your gifts of resources, you are priceless. Thank you! I know there are many more who I have not named who have prayed along the way for this study. Thank you from the bottom of my heart.

To my sweet husband, Gordon, who never once complained about dinner or the lack there of, or the late hours. You have always supported me in everything I have done. I love you so much and I am so proud to be your wife. As for my sweet pea, Taylor, you are my joy! Thank you for your understanding of the many hours of working on this project, especially the last three weeks. You truly are the best kid ever!! I love you so much, and even more than that.

But most of all, to you, Lord. I am so undeserving of your great love and grace. You truly have stolen my heart! Thank you for the privilege and responsibility to move my passion of teaching your Word to a different level. I pray that every woman who reads this study will want to know you more and have a faith that becomes ignited, and will strive to glorify you in everything she does for the rest of her life.

To God be the glory, great things He hath done!

Praising Him!

Much love to all, Tanya

Introduction
❧❧❧

Have you ever been walking along in your relationship with God and then all of the sudden—wham-o!—something happens? Your cheese gets knocked off your cracker.

How can you walk along, filled with joy, singing, raising your hands at worship, serving, praying, having all kinds of Spirit-filled thoughts and actions, to wondering if God even cares about what is going on in your life. Or maybe you have been so full of doubt and discouragement that you are not willing to make an effort to press on anymore, no matter what the circumstance. You are tired of trying so hard.

I have been on that journey. I did the three-step program to becoming a spiritual giant: I read His word every day, prayed every day, and served Him every day. I was sure I had "Christian of the Year" all sown up! I even wallowed in the "I am not Second, but 42nd" attitude. Look at poor, humble me!

It wasn't one particular day, it wasn't one particular moment; it was a slow fade. Even my passion of His word and teaching, which drives me so, was declining at a rapid speed, and I wasn't sure why. Or maybe I knew why but wasn't ready for others to see this wounded warrior. To be honest, I was walking wounded and didn't realize it.

On this journey, many days were partly-cloudy but most were dark-and-dreary. I couldn't stand myself. Ever been in that position? The self-pity was so damaging to me and to those around me. This type of journey was new to me, and my thoughts and actions were out of character. I was on a battlefield I hadn't seen before and not as equipped as I should have been.

I asked God many questions about this new battle. However, I did get to a point where I stopped asking and just started resting in Him. Resting in Him is not action enough for me, if you know what I mean. I am a professional list-maker and doer. But after many months, with much learned and still to be learned on this journey, our faithful God led me to several insights. I must share these learned insights from this journey, or I will bust. Much like Jeremiah.

Writing/teaching studies and developing Bible study leaders is my passion. I claim the verse Jeremiah 20:9, NLT:

> But if I say I'll never mention the Lord or speak in His name, His word burns in my heart like a fire. It's like a fire in my bones! I am worn out trying to hold it in! I can't do it!

I find it interesting how God used Jeremiah to explain my passion of igniting faith in others and to also help me understand this journey.

Jeremiah was a prophet, but for the sake of this study, let's call him a Warrior. His life was very difficult but he still loved and obeyed the Lord. At one point, Jeremiah was crying to God about how he was being treated unfairly. I am sure he was discouraged even as he was being obedient to God. In Jeremiah 12:5, after Jeremiah has done all his whining, God basically says, "Jeremiah, this is nothing. Things will get worse. Consider this training for the real battle. Let's get through this one; learn and grow and become strong, so you won't be destroyed on the next journey."

At this point, Jeremiah was a Broken Warrior. Jeremiah was full of passion for the Lord but still faced much heartache from being rejected, imprisoned, physically abused, and more. Jeremiah had to depend on God's love as he developed endurance. I haven't faced the heartaches Jeremiah experienced, and you might not have either to that extent, but while doubt, discouragement, loneliness, and esteem issues can be shot from different bows, they have the same piercing effect. As a fellow Broken Warrior, I bet you have been crying on the inside and nobody knows it but you and God. I bet you smile and keep moving, when you desperately just want to lie down and not get up. Let me encourage you by saying it is okay to drop your sword and rest in our Lord. God promises us a plan to prosper us and not to harm us. He has plans to give us hope and a future. Jeremiah tells us that too.

I pray these pages of insight will encourage you. I pray as you read this study you will remain open to God's leading and be willing to put your complete trust in Him. I pray your relationship with our

Lord becomes so strong and passionate that your faith will be ignited to not only change your life, but also influence other lives.

My friend, I can hardly wait to hear how God will work in your life, as a renewed and restored Broken Warrior.

Chapter 1
ఈఈఈ

I Heard it Through the Grapevine

"I am the vine, you are the branches. If a man remains in me and I in him, he will bear much fruit; apart from me you can do nothing" (John 15:5).

When I was a kid, the house we lived in had a large backyard. The good news was it housed a beautiful Weeping Willow tree. The bad news was that it was a switch-producing Weeping Willow tree. When my brother would get in trouble, he had to cut his own branch off this tree and then remove the leaves. This process produced the "please don't hit me with it" switch. This switch was swatted once or twice across the legs when you had done something wrong. I was told that it stung. That's right, I never had to experience "The Switch," it was always my older brother. Ha-ha. However, one day I was summoned to cut off a willow branch, even though I was sure my brother was the culprit who got me in trouble. Being a brilliant six year old, I returned with a tiny three-inch switch. "*How could this possibly hurt me?*" I thought. The disciplinary action continued right on track, even with a three-inch branch. More importantly, I saw that the switch cutting was a significant part of the process.

This chapter doesn't discuss the switch-making process, but does enlighten us about a sometimes painful pruning process. We will also discover the joys of "remaining in Him." I pray you read the following chapter with an open heart and mind and let God renew and restore you.

Cutting Branches

John records many things Jesus taught. For example, in John 15, verses 1-8, Jesus is teaching us, as believers, that while we are privileged to share His life, we also are expected to abide/remain in Him. That is our responsibility. Jesus is very clear in this scripture. Let's take a look:

> *"I am the true vine, and my Father is the gardener. He cuts off every branch in me that bears no fruit, while every branch that does bear fruit He prunes so that it will be even more fruitful. You are already clean because of the word I have spoken to you. Remain in me, and I will remain in you. No branch can bear fruit by itself; it must remain in the vine. Neither can you bear fruit unless you remain in me. "I am the vine; you are the branches. If a man remains in me and I in him, he will bear much fruit; apart from me you can do nothing"* (John 15:1-5).

2

The way Jesus taught excites me. He gave such great illustrations, and was so quick minded. We see His great teaching in this passage. We pick up the story here where Jesus and His disciples had just left the Upper Room in Jerusalem and were walking to the Garden of Gethsemane. Jesus would soon be arrested and crucified. Now, I would think He would be preoccupied with His upcoming demise, but instead passed through a vineyard and used the comparison of the vine and branches to teach His disciples even more lessons.

In this vineyard illustration, Jesus is the vine; God is the vinedresser; and we, the believers are the branches.

Now let's educate ourselves a little about the vineyard and the vinedresser so we can try to put ourselves in the story to help us understand what Jesus was teaching. First, the main purpose of the grapevine is to produce grapes. In order to produce this fruit, pruning is a necessary process. Because the pruning process of the vineyard was common knowledge in those days, Jesus knew the disciples would understand His illustration.

 Another fact worth noting is grapevines are pruned way back for the first three years to keep them from bearing fruit; this way they can produce quality grapes later on.

Pruning is done with a tool which has a hook and a sharp curved blade. Fruitless and dead branches are found and cut off. And the reason for the cutting is so the life-giving sap from the vine can flow to the fruit-bearing branches. If the branches are not pruned, they can become useless, dead. However, if some branches are not cut off, this can be damaging to the other branches as well.

God, our vinedresser, knows what we need and don't need. He knows what branches need to be cut off. Sometimes these branches may look pretty good to us and even bear fruit. This type of pruning can be painful, but take encouragement. Lawrence O. Richards says: "*God is fully committed to bring us to maximum fruitfulness. God's pruning work benefits us; it doesn't threaten us.*"

These words from Bruce Wilkerson's book, *Secrets of the Vine*, really struck a chord with me. He explains, "growers prune their vineyards more intensively as the vines age. The vine's ability to produce growth increases each year, but without intensive pruning the plant weakens and its crop diminishes. Mature branches must be pruned hard to achieve maximum yields."

I know, I didn't like what he said, either.

In other words, if the grape plant is left to itself, it will always favor new growth over more grapes. So from a distance, you see luxurious growth. Up close, you see an underwhelming harvest. This is why the vinedresser cuts away unnecessary shoots, no matter how vigorous, because the vineyard's only purpose, their "*one thing*," is grapes.

What are you being pruned for? What is your "*one thing*"? In the book *The Leadership Secrets of Billy Graham* by Harold Myra, he explains Billy Graham was pruned for his "*one thing.*" You don't have to be a Christian to be familiar with the name Billy Graham. Billy Graham's tremendous impact on thousands resulted from the pruning for "his one thing"---evangelism. You might even be in the family of God because of him.

Warrior Weapon

God prunes me to benefit me, not to harm me

Let Go of the Branch

My last pruning session was very painful and instead of sitting and letting God cut away the branches He deemed necessary, I kept using my "try to catch me" maneuvers. I kept picturing myself as a child put in the time-out chair to sit, but anxiously and impatiently waiting to get up the whole time. I was like the child who told her Mom "I may be sitting down on the outside, but I am standing up on the inside!" One day, God took me by both shoulders, placed me on the chair, and said in His deep, booming voice, "Tanya, I said sit down." Well, His voice wasn't really deep and booming; I just added that for effect. But in my Spirit, He was saying, "My child, sit down, be still, and know that I am God."

Could it be possible you are going through a pruning process and don't know it? Honestly, I didn't realize at first I was in the pruning process. It wasn't until after I had spent some time praying, asking, complaining, crying, reading, and seeking wise counsel that I finally understood what was going on. During this time of pruning, some days were pretty dark, but our sweet gracious God would always give enough light to sustain me.

At lunch one day, I bought my trusty little sandwich, cookie, and drink. As I headed for home, I changed my mind unexpectedly and drove to a local prayer garden. What a great idea, I thought...lunch in the garden with just God and me. As I pulled up to the garden, I could see a worker, a woman, tending to the soil and fixing the landscape. No one else there. Even though I was glad, the presence of the worker bothered me because I was hoping for this time to just be mine. (Selfish, I know. The pruning can really make you feel sorry for yourself). Anyway, as I approached the worker, I then realized it was Brenda. I had met Brenda several years ago. Brenda is the owner of the Prayer Garden, an author, teacher, and definitely what one would call "wise counsel." It was not part of her plan to be there that day nor was it mine. Yet, the "light" I received from being in the garden that day, was priceless.

As I walked up to her, I said, "Brenda, remember me?" She said, "Tanya, of course." And then her mistake was what she said next. "How are you?" Well, for the next hour we walked around the garden while I talked her ear off about my spiritual journey. I explained the confusion I felt about my growth. She shared words of wisdom and her story of a similar journey; this was so encouraging to me. As I described my journey, I explained I had been through the pruning process before but this time was different. The next words she spoke to me as we stood in the shade of the garden, rang a sound I could understand. She said, "Tanya, it is easy to put yourself on the cross, because you can get down anytime you want to but..." Just then I clearly understood I was being pruned. What a great metaphor my friend used. I would need to learn patience, endure the pruning and wait for God's perfect timing to finish cutting the worthless branches off, even the ones which appeared fruitful. (I'm not sure about you, but sitting and waiting are really not my strengths. I have tried asking God for more patience, but I always want it NOW!)

Well as the pruning continued, I can't say I understood why He cut some branches, but I have finally came to the conclusion I don't need to understand why God does what He does. Having to understand why God does things is prideful. Think about it.   Didn't Eve eat the fruit because she wanted to be like God, to know what God knows? Yikes! We know what happened to Eve.

The good news is, God is with us during the pruning process. God wants nothing more than to bless us and to give us abundant life. Ask yourself this question. Are you hanging onto branches that are really sucking the life out of other branches which could be extremely fruitful? Are you hanging onto branches that jeopardize your "one thing?"

Trust God during this process. Why? Because...

"He cuts off every branch in me that bears no fruit, while every branch that does bear fruit He prunes so that it will be even more fruitful" (John 15:2).

Warrior Weapon

Let God cut the branches He deems necessary, even if I think they are good branches.

Remain, Remain, Remain

We have a great dog, a Sheltie, named Luke. Luke is smart, and obedient, and as I always tell him, "the best dog ever." Luke loves me no matter what and that's why he is typically my favorite in the family. Luke learned quickly who feeds him, pets him, plays with him, and on a lot of occasions, talks to him. Luke knows who his master is. When I tell him to sit and stay, or let's say, "sit and remain", Luke then gets a treat. He loves treats. Treats bring him joy and non-stop tail wagging. Oh to be as smart as Luke.

As we continue in our passage of John 15:5, we see we are to act like Luke (the dog), to remain, stay with our Master.

"I am the vine, you are the branches, if a man remains in me and I in him, he will bear much fruit; apart from me, you can do nothing."

In this verse, Jesus is trying to get us to sit and stay. He tells us we will get a treat if we do. But you see, to "remain in Him" requires a commitment on our part. However, this is made possible because of the given gift of the Holy Spirit dwelling in us. As a growing disciple, we must be continuously connected to Christ: He is the vine.

The last part of verse 5 is clear in every translation, "*you can do nothing.*" The verse does not end with "you can do nothing, sometimes," or "you cannot do as well." The words are clear, the intent is clear, "*apart from me, (Jesus) you can do nothing*!"

I believe the end of the verse, *apart from me*, is a glimpse of what we would be like if it were not for Him. Oswald Chambers, in *My Utmost for His Highest*, asks: "Do I long to be so closely identified with Jesus that I am of no value for anything except Him and His purposes?"

I am convinced God's silence during my journey was to give me a look back at my "old way of life." I knew He was with me every step but the reminder of being apart from Him I could do nothing, was such a blessing to me. Well, it wasn't at first. I knew God was doing what was best for me, but it wasn't easy remaining while He pruned. I am sure glad God surrounded me with prayer warrior friends. Asking friends to pray for you is invaluable.

Again, the illustration of the vine and branches being like our relationship with Jesus, is brilliant. On a grapevine, you can't tell where the vine ends and the branch begins. This is exactly what Jesus wants for His followers. We are to remain in Him so closely others will see Jesus through us.

In *Secrets of the Vine*, Bruce Wilkinson writes, "Abiding (remaining) is all about the most important friendship of your life. More abiding means more of God in your life, more of Him in your activities, thoughts, and desires."

After you meet with God in the morning, take Him with you everywhere. I know this sounds simple, but we tend to make this an activity we schedule into our day as opposed to REMAINING with Him. Since God is with us always, our abiding is continual. God is not a season, an appointment, or a once-a-week activity.

> *Your fellowship with God does not necessarily guarantee a good day; but it does guarantee that you can get through the day to the glory of God.*
> *Cynthia Heald*

One day a Preacher was driving on a beautiful curvy country road when he got into the rhythm of the car in front of him. The preacher started watching the car so intensely that he would swerve when the car in front swerved. This continued for several miles, swerving, driving reckless, going faster, and slowing down. Finally, as the car in front took a curve much too fast, the preacher did too but didn't make the turn, flying off into a ditch. The car in front saw the preacher go off the road, stopped, turned around, and went to find out if he was okay. The first driver got out of his car, stumbling due to alcohol consumption, and leaned over the preacher's car, words slurred as he asked, "Heeyy Buddyy, are you okay? The preacher replied in his resonant pulpit tone, "Yes, my son...for the Lord is riding with me." The drunk then replied with concern, "That's greeaaat, but you better let Him ride with me because you are gonna get Him killed!"

Is God riding with you every day, throughout your day?

Will you spend time getting to know your Creator, your Prince of Peace? Remain in Him. God doesn't want to be **part** of your life; **He wants to be your life.**

Warrior Weapon

To remain in Him all day, every day so others won't know where He ends and I begin.

Fill'er Up

Remaining in Him. Others will start seeing Jesus through us as they witness His love, His thoughts, and His ways.

John tells the story of a Samaritan woman at a well who encounters Jesus as she draws water. He fills her with "living water." What Jesus meant by filling with living water is clarified in John 7:37-39:

> *On the last and greatest day of the Feast, Jesus stood and said in a loud voice, If a man is thirsty, let him come to me and drink. Whoever believes in me, as the Scripture has said, streams of living water will flow from within him. "*

Being filled with Jesus is not a one-time event. It's a moment-by-moment way of life. Andrew Murray says: "Man's glory and blessedness was not to be independent, or dependent upon himself, but dependent on God. Man was to have the joy of receiving every moment out of the fullness of God." One of the keys to remaining in Him is *letting* yourself be filled up with His living water: Love,Joy, Peace, Patience, Kindness, Goodness, Faithfulness, Gentleness and Self-Control. When you are "filled up," you can pour out Him to others. You can be Jesus with skin on. However, sometimes we let ourselves run dry, with nothing to pour out. And sometimes God can't or won't pour in.

In Bible days, wine was stored in bags made out of goat-skins. When new wine is poured into the wineskin, it expands because of fermentation, stretching the wineskin. So if you pour new wine into an old bag, the wine will not only become sour, but the wineskin will burst. Therefore, one needs to put new wine into new wineskins.

"And no one puts new wine into old wineskins. For the old skins would burst from the pressure, spilling the wine and ruining the skins. New wine is stored in new wineskins so that both are preserved" (Matthew 9:17).

Again, Jesus is such a brilliant teacher. He is using a familiar common practice to teach as he speaks to the Religious leaders. How does this apply to you and me?

Think of yourself as the "wineskin" in this verse. We can only hold His fresh, living water. Sometimes we fill our wineskins with worldly, temporary things. Just like the Samaritan woman who thought having a man (5 husbands) would make her happy. She was looking for love in all the wrong places until she met Jesus. This woman LET Jesus fill her up. What are you counting on to fill you up? Is it money, a perfect family, the perfect house, a man, a career?

Here are some questions to ask yourself to see if you, the vessel, can receive some insight as to why your wineskin is not being filled to capacity or at all.

*Is God trying to fill me up and this wineskin is dirty?

*Is something blocking the filling? (Lack of forgiveness)

*Was I filled up with something other than Him?

Warrior Weapon

Examine daily what might be blocking the filling of Christ in me. Pray Psalm 139:23-24, "Search me, O God, and know my heart, test me and know my anxious thoughts. Point out anything in me that offends you, and lead me along the path of everlasting life."

Perfect submission, all is at rest,
I in my Savior am happy and blest;
Watching and waiting, looking above,
Filled with His goodness, lost in His love.

Preparing for Battle
ぁぁぁ

Write the scripture John 16:33

_____

_____

_____

Write the scripture Romans 8:31

_____

_____

_____

If you were to prune yourself, what would be the first branch you would cut off?   Why?

_____

_____

_____

Examine the last year of your spiritual walk. Do you see where God cut off some branches so you would produce bigger and better grapes? What branch did He cut off?

_____

_____

_____

What does "remaining in Him" look like to you?

_____

_____

_____

What can you add, change, or remove from your daily life to help you "remain" in Him?

_____

_____

_____

Ask yourself, are you being filled up every day, overflowing with His love, so much it pours out into others. Or is there something blocking this filling? If so, what is the blockage?

_____

_____

_____

What is one way the world's advice differs from Jesus' in John 15:4? What makes you think that you are attached to the vine?

_____

_____

_____

Why is it important to be deliberate about our intention to be close to Jesus Christ?

_____

_____

_____

What is the ultimate purpose for bearing fruit?

_____

_____

_____

What does this passage, John 15:1-8, tell you about Jesus?

_____

_____

_____

Weapons of Truth

Memorize:

"I am the vine, you are the branches. If a man remains in me and I in him, he will bear much fruit; apart from me you can do nothing" (John 15:5).

Digging Deeper

Read John 15: 1-8 in several translations.

What words were emphasized and/or repeated?

_____

_____

_____

Why do you think these words were emphasized and/or repeated?

_____

_____

_____

Is there a promise in this passage you can claim? If so, write it down. Maybe start a book of promises.

_____

_____

_____

To whom, was Jesus telling this parable? Did Judas Iscariot hear this message? How do you know?

_____

_____

_____

Do a concordance search on the word "remain" and see what other scriptures support this message.

_____

_____

_____

Why do you think Jesus said what He did in John 15:3?

_____

_____

_____

Further reading

Secrets of the Vine by Bruce Wilkinson. This is a small, quick, excellent read.

Chapter 2
ॐॐॐ

Help Me, I'm Drowning

"The LORD himself goes before you and will be with you; He will never leave you nor forsake you. Do not be afraid; do not be discouraged" (Deuteronomy 31:8).

"Knock, Knock." "Who's there?" "Dwayne." "Dwayne who?" "Dwayne the bathtub, I'm Dwowning."

I remember telling this joke when I was five years old. And at age five, it was a real crowd pleaser; now, maybe not so much. The reality of the joke now is instead of water, Dwayne could be drowning in a bathtub of unpaid bills, health issues, legal issues, emotional issues. I could be Dwayne; you could be Dwayne.

Drowning in a tub of disappointment, discouragement and depression is debilitating. Worse yet, you can't seem to reach the plug to give yourself some relief. I pray this chapter will lead you to an empty tub as you discover God's truths.

The Three Ds

I don't think you have to look too hard to find many who are drowning in discouragement. I have a friend whose child has an unceasing appetite for drugs. The waves of discouragement come over causing her deep depression. Another friend who just can't seem to keep her head above water financially and her discouragement is keeping her from even trying to budget. Maybe your discouragement waves come from trying to hold your marriage together. Just when you think you are making progress, another wave slams into you and knocks you down, but this time you don't want to get up and try again. Maybe it is a dream you have worked toward, but keep falling short. Or maybe it is health issues. You are finally feeling better, when you find out another surgery is needed. Often the direct hit of a wave of discouragement comes from another's words, or lack thereof.

These feelings of despair can and do happen to everyone. Nobody is unbreakable here on this earth. Even if you have done "everything right," you are not exempt from the waves of the Three D's.

To summarize: the greater the hope, the desire, and the expectation, the greater the disappointment.

Disappointment ---->Discouragement ---->Depression

When we come to know Jesus, we don't instantly become free of negative emotions or thoughts. But, we do have the chance and choice to experience freedom from these thoughts and emotions and the freedom to become everything God intends for us to be, living life to the fullest (John 10:10). Between prayer, praise and His word, we can learn to accept His love and His freedom and unlock the chains of negative emotions which bind us.

Negative thoughts tend to block our acceptance of God's love and peace. Now I am not saying if you just think positive everything will be great. What I am saying is we must come to an understanding of our thoughts and emotions. Specifically, how it affects the Three D's.

Disappointment/Discouragement

Let's start with disappointment. We can sum up this feeling, in two words; *projected expectations*. Projected expectations are when **you** project what you think someone should say or do, or expect a situation to be how you imagined. When these expectations are not met, disappointment enters, and can come in a mighty way. The greater the hope and desire; the greater the disappointment.

Instead of dealing with our disappointments as they come, we obsess over them. I'm not sure why except it gives us reason to put the light on ourselves in a weird, twisted way. We then start becoming accustomed to damaging thoughts and they begin to taint everything we say and do.

These thoughts are fire starters for feelings of disappointment. And those sparks fuel the fire of discouragement.

Now before we go any further, please understand these negative emotions are not God's will for your life. You might be saying, "Well I am not a positive person, this is just the way I am."

God did not make you "that" way. God knows the damaging effects of negative thoughts. If you have accepted Christ, you now have the opportunity and power to transform your mind and heart.

> "*Those who get up and spend time in the Word to begin the day are not devoid of problems; they're not devoid of discouragement. They just get over it quicker.*" Billy Graham

Warrior Weapon

"*Ask God to bring my soul out of prison, that I may praise Your name*" (Psalm 142:7).

I wondered if being a "people pleaser" might catapult us into one of the Three D's? Or what about trying to please God? Don't you think this starts the "Maybe God forgives me, but I just can't forgive myself" syndrome.

We just keep playing our thoughts or actions over and over and over again so much, it wears grooves in our thinking. Our thoughts spin out of control, moving in the wrong direction.

2 Corinthians 10:5 tells us;

"We are destroying speculations and every lofty thing raised up against the knowledge of God, and we are taking every thought captive to the obedience of Christ" (NASB).

Depression

Depression hit me hard about 18 years ago. It was triggered by disappointment, which led to extreme discouragement and eventually the emotional death of depression. My husband and I went through 5 years of infertility. My projected expectations were to have a family. When that didn't happen the way I had planned, and I was disappointed month after month, I hit an all time low of discouragement. I didn't understand why I wasn't given a child. Others around me, who didn't even want children, were having them.

Ever wanted something desperately and you thought you were deserving, so you come to the conclusion, "God must be punishing me." I know that doesn't sound right, but I am betting there are many of you who are in a situation and you are thinking the same thing. Of course this opened many doors of other negative thoughts and emotions, which led me into depression.

Please don't misunderstand me when we talk about depression, I know depression is real. There is such a thing as biochemical imbalance depression. And there is nothing wrong with taking medication. But typically most depressions are rooted in emotional factors.

During the time of my infertility, I was a believer, just not a true follower of Jesus. Unfortunately, I was not aware of the equipping and empowering available to help me endure this battle. However, God did use this trial to bring me back to Him in a mighty way. (Romans 8:28)

Don't get me wrong, I am not saying we will live in 24 hour "bliss." There are times when we are fearful, full of anxiety. Or God leads us down an unknown path and it is scary. That can be very discouraging. Or when we don't see a " way out" of a situation or even a "way in," and then we become disappointed, discouraged, depressed.

Watchman Nee says it perfectly:

> *"Painful indeed you may find it, but the blessing you need is behind it."*

There is a story in the Bible in first Samuel, Chapter 1, about a woman named Hannah. Hannah could be our poster child for the Three D's, however, she also leads us to the solution.

A Bad Penny

In the first book of Samuel, Chapter 1, we learn about a woman whose disappointment and discouragement leads her to depression. Her name is Hannah, a Broken Warrior. Hannah was married to Elkanah, as was Peninnah. Here lies the first problem:

one man, two wives. That would be enough to send anyone into depression. But it was not uncommon in those days to have more than one wife. As we read this chapter we see that Peninnah had children but Hannah had none.

2 He had two wives; one was called Hannah and the other Peninnah. Peninnah had children, but Hannah had none. 4 Whenever the day came for Elkanah to sacrifice, he would give portions of the meat to his wife Peninnah and to all her sons and daughters. 5 But to Hannah he gave a double portion because he loved her, and the LORD had closed her womb. 6 And because the LORD had closed her womb, her rival kept provoking her in order to irritate her. 7 This went on year after year. Whenever Hannah went up to the house of the LORD, her rival provoked her till she wept and would not eat. 8 Elkanah her husband would say to her, "Hannah, why are you weeping? Why don't you eat? Why are you downhearted? Don't I mean more to you than ten sons?" 12 As she kept on praying to the LORD, Eli observed her mouth. 13 Hannah was praying in her heart, and her lips were moving but her voice was not heard. Eli thought she was drunk 14 and said to her, "How long will you keep on getting drunk? Get rid of your wine." 15 "Not so, my lord," Hannah replied, "I am a woman who is deeply troubled. I have not been drinking wine or beer; I was pouring out my soul to the LORD. 16 Do not take your servant for a wicked woman; I have been praying here out of my great anguish and grief."

(Have you ever let out a scream or cry out of anguish because it was all you could do?)

17 Eli answered, "Go in peace, and may the God of Israel grant you what you have asked of Him." 18 She said, "May your servant find favor in your eyes." Then she went her way and ate something, and her face was no longer downcast.

In Hannah's days it was a disgrace to be barren. Not being able to produce children was considered to be a useless link in the chain leading to the promised Messiah. OUCH! Elkanah probably married Peninnah—possibly from the urging of Hannah, as Sarah did with Abraham—just for the reason of bearing children. Apparently, Peninnah, let's call her Penny, was fertile Myrtle.

As you read this passage you see disappointment and discouragement has really set in for Hannah (v 7-8,15). She wanted a child desperately. Penny, the other wife, had what Hannah wanted. Being the bad Penny she was, she rubbed it in Hannah's face daily. Penny made Hannah cry, not eat, feel downhearted, and depressed. I don't know about you but I would like to put Ms. Penny in the wood chipper.

Ever notice when you want something desperately, and you see others who have what you want, this leads quickly to the Three D's. Do you wonder what Hannah was thinking at this point? I wonder if Hannah thought she had done something wrong to anger God or not done something right to make the Lord close her womb? As you read on, the story has a happy ending. Hannah's prayer for a child was answered. However, Hannah also lived up to her promise of "If you give us a son, we will give him back to you" (v 11).

Hannah is a great example of a basic principle of the Christian life. Mark 8:35,

> *"For whoever wants to save his life will lose it, but whoever loses his life for me and for the gospel will save it."*

Here is the warning label: when our prayers are answered, we must not let the gift received become more important than the Giver. Why? Because when we are not thankful, and become complacent with God and His gifts, we don't give the gift back to Him, this can become a stumbling block in our lives. Our possessions, our abilities, our family, our plans, our hurts, our minds, must be placed at His feet to bless them to use for His glory. God did answer Hannah's plea, when she poured her heart out to Him. Being a woman of faith, Hannah went through with her promise to give her son back to God. She really did, literally by giving him to Eli for temple service. I am thinking maybe Hannah was clinging to the promise of "rejoicing comes in the morning." Psalm 30:5

The rejoicing may come the morning after the night of crying and pleading with God. Or the morning after a wrestling match with God about what you will lay on the altar for Him to use. I don't know when your morning of rejoicing will come but I do know the morning of rejoicing is coming!

> *"...weeping may remain for a night, but rejoicing comes in the morning"* (Psalm 30:5).

What can we learn from Hannah?

Along with encouragement from the priest and nourishment for her body, Hannah's face was no longer downcast. Her depression had lifted. At this point she didn't know if God would answer her prayer or not.

1. Hannah sought God when she was in her deepest distress and knew only He could answer her questions, providing her comfort and her purpose in life.

2. She responded to her disappointments by praying. She took the focus off of herself, and put it all on God.

3. Her depression lifted because she poured out her heart to God.

    a. Our tendency is to cry to others, or bring them down with us. She made God her first resort-not last.

4. She had self-control. Although Hannah could have knocked the "dog" out of Peninnah, she didn't.

5. She gave God all the Glory and Praise.
    a. Her prayer is recorded in Chapter 2:1-10.
    b. She recognizes God's Holiness.
        i. His perfect knowledge keeps Him from doing anything in our lives not perfectly right for us.
        ii. This should give us confidence in His action in our lives.

First Samuel 2:1-10 is Hannah's prayer of praise to God. Read this prayer in your Bible. Notice how she praised God. Hannah saw God as solid as a rock. Basically this prayer is really a song of praise she sang to the Lord. It tells of God's grace, about His joy, God's victory over the enemy, and the wonderful way He turns things around to accomplish His purposes. One more thing worth noting, which needs to be said in bold and caps:

HANNAH LEFT HER PROBLEMS WITH GOD

Even though Hannah was lifted from depression and regained her strength, she didn't go back and pick everything up again she had just cried out to God about. **She had faith, trusted God, and left her problems at the altar.** Now that is something we all need to learn. I would call Hannah a renewed and restored Broken Warrior, wouldn't you?

Warrior Weapon

As Broken Warriors we will "Go to the throne and not the phone." Go to God first and honestly, with faith and trust, then to others who will encourage us and not feed the discouragement. Give God all the Glory and Praise, no matter what the outcome.

Before we go on, I just have to say something about Peninnah. Penny was a woman conquered by jealousy. Penny allowed her bitterness to take root in her heart. I am thinking Penny must have had some projected expectations, disappointment, and discouragement had tainted her heart. As a result, her life became poisoned with envy. Jealousy can devour a person. Many of us have people like Penny in our lives, someone who is abrasive and difficult to live with or work with. Penny never once saw Hannah's broken heart. There is much we can learn from Peninnah as well.

The Three Ps

When you are in the darkness of discouragement, you tend to lose your direction, your hopes, dreams, and perspective. After so many disappointments you begin to fear putting your hope and hard work into anything, right? It is much easier to complain and wallow in self-pity, to not get close to anyone, or move forward with anything, to stand 'like a deer in headlights' than to risk being hurt again.

Maybe one way of battling our negative emotions is to change the direction of our thinking, to view life like this: *God is not something we add to our life, God IS our life.* What if we lived to worship our God and then added family, possessions, etc? What do you think this perspective on everyday life would mean for you?

It is time to re-direct, re-focus, much like Hannah did. Hopefully you will gain insight as to how to dig out of the three Ds by using the Three Ps. Praise, Prayer, and Press On.

Praise

"Be joyful always; pray continually; give thanks in all circumstances, for this is God's will for you in Christ Jesus" (1 Thessalonians 5:16-18).

You may be puzzled about what it means to praise continually and give thanks always, in every situation. It is easy to praise God when everything is going great. But let's say you don't feel thankful about your circumstances. Ever felt like that before? The Bible commands us to *give thanks in all circumstances*. God is a Big God; we are the ones who make Him small. We make Him small by not thinking we can be honest with Him and cry to Him. But God knows everything in our hearts and how we feel. It doesn't mean we deny our negative thoughts and feelings. We just don't let them control us. We are to come to God with everything, completely honest like Hannah or even honest and whiney like David in Psalms. David was a real cry baby besides being a murderer and adulterer. And still, God said he was man after His own heart.

We see examples of the psalmists expressing their feelings, still choosing to praise in spite of how things seemed. When we follow these examples, typically the Lord will release us from being a slave to our distressing emotions. He may not answer our questions about how He will handle our problems, but rest, my fellow Broken Warrior, in His many promises of faithfulness. Hannah did. She did not have an answer when she finished praying, but her depression was lifted.

On my dark days, even though it is not easy, I sit until I can write something in my Praise Journal. One day, in my cave of darkness I finished my loud and not-so-edifying speech to the family, including the cat and dog, of "I have to do everything around here, no one helps me, nobody cares but me...blah, blah, blah." You know the rest of that speech. But, I could still say "Lord, you know my heart. I don't understand right now how I am to be thankful for this situation I am in, but I will trust You and thank You, for Your love endures forever."

Pray also for a *lifestyle of praise* and for your mind to be filled with His thoughts and not yours. This may take some time but if you will choose to cultivate the habit of praise, I know God will enrich your praise life and you will be pleasantly surprised.

One of my favorite passages is in 2 Chronicles 20:1-30. To summarize: war was declared on King Jehoshaphat because he was trying to instill God's ways and laws in Jerusalem, but several of the surrounding towns didn't like it. They declared war on Jehoshaphat. When he finds out about the impending battle, he immediately seeks the Lord's help. Then he stands up in front of the people of Judah and Jerusalem at the temple and begins praising the Lord. God, being the compassionate God He is, gives Jehoshaphat encouragement throughout this passage. Telling him things such as:

> *"Do not be afraid or discouraged because of this vast army. For the battle is not yours, but God's."*

> *"Do not be afraid, do not be discouraged. Go out to face them tomorrow, and the Lord will be with you."*

Jehoshaphat then bowed his face to the ground and praised God. Now listen to this: the next day as they went to battle, Jehoshaphat appointed men to sing to the Lord and to praise Him for the splendor of His holiness as they went out at the front of the army. Did you get that? Jehoshaphat did not send the best warriors, not the biggest warriors, not even warriors who were armed, but rather men appointed to sing and shout praises to the Lord. They went ahead of the army saying:

"Give thanks to the Lord, for His love endures forever."

Next we start to see God, as my mom would say, "really showing out." As the men began to sing and praise, the Lord set ambushes against the bad guys. They even turned on each other and destroyed one another. When Jehoshaphat and his men arrived, there was no battle to fight. God had taken care of it. And if that wasn't enough to shout praises about, it took three days to collect all the things of value, much equipment, clothing, etc. Still, there is one more treasure God left them with in verse 30: "*And the kingdom of Jehoshaphat was at peace, for his God had given him rest on every side.*" God even gave them rest. How perfect is all that?

Make praise a part of your everyday life. Please see the homework section in the back of this chapter for more guidance on starting your own Praise Journal.

When you are having one of those days where you can't find anything to be thankful for, or just don't feel like it, maybe the following story will help.

Sandra, a Broken Warrior, was drowning in discouragement when she opened the florist shop door. Her life had been as sweet as a spring breeze and then in the fourth month of her second pregnancy, a "minor" car accident stole her joy.

This was Easter week and the time she should have delivered their infant son. She grieved over their loss. Troubles had multiplied. Her husband's company was threatening layoffs. Her sister had called and said she couldn't come for the long-awaited visit. And her long-time companion Sheltie dog had just died. What was worse is that a friend suggested to Sandra that maybe her grief was a God-given path to maturity which would allow her to empathize with others who suffer. "She has no idea what I'm feeling," thought Sandra.

Here it was Easter and she knew she should be thankful for what God had done for her, but how could she be thankful for the careless driver whose truck was hardly scratched when he rear-ended her? For an airbag that saved her life, but took her child's?

"Good afternoon, can I help you?" Sandra was startled by the approach of the shop clerk.

"I...I need an arrangement," Sandra said with a lump in her throat.

"For Easter? Do you want the beautiful but ordinary, or would you like to challenge the day with a customer favorite I call the Easter Special?

"I'm convinced flowers tell stories," she continued. "Are you looking for something that conveys gratitude this Easter?"

"Not exactly!" Sandra blurted out. "In the last five months, everything that could go wrong has gone wrong." Looking down, Sandra regretted her outburst but was surprised when the clerk said, "I have the perfect arrangement for you."

Then the bell on the door rang, and the clerk greeted the new customer. "Hi Barbara...let me get your order." She excused herself and walked back to a small workroom, then quickly reappeared, carrying an arrangement of greenery, bows, and what appeared to be long-stemmed thorny roses. EXCEPT the ends of the rose stems were snipped, there were no flowers.

"Do you want this in a box?" asked the clerk. Sandra watched for the customer's response. Was this a joke? Who would want rose stems with no flowers! She waited for laugher, but neither woman laughed. "Yes, please," Barbara replied with an appreciative smile. "You'd think after three years of getting the Special, I wouldn't be so moved by its significance, but I can feel it right here, all over again," she said as she gently tapped her chest.

Sandra stammered, "Ah, that lady just left with, uh...she left with no flowers!"

"That's right, said the clerk. "I cut off the flowers. That's the Special. I call it the Easter Thorns Bouquet."

"Oh, come on! You can't tell me someone is willing to pay for that!" exclaimed Sandra.

"Barbara came into the shop three years ago, feeling much as you do today," explained the clerk. "She thought she had very little to be thankful for. She had just lost her father to cancer, the family business was failing, her son had gotten into drugs, and she was facing major surgery.

"That same year I had lost my husband," continued the clerk. "For the first time in my life, I had to spend the holidays alone. I had no children, no husband, no family nearby, and too much debt to allow any travel."

"So what did you do?" asked Sandra.

"I learned to be thankful for the thorns," answered the clerk quietly.

"I've always thanked God for the good things in my life and I never asked Him why those GOOD things happened to me, but when the bad stuff hit, I cried out, 'WHY, WHY ME?!' It took time for me to learn the dark times are important to our faith. I have always enjoyed the "Flowers" of my life, but it took the thorns to show me the beauty of God's comfort! You know, the Bible says that God comforts us when we're afflicted, and from His consolation we learn to comfort others."

Sandra took a deep breath, as she thought about what her friend had told her. "I guess the truth is I don't want comfort. I've lost a baby and I'm angry with God!"

Just then someone else walked in the shop. "Hey Phil," the clerk greeted the man.

"My wife sent me in to get our usual Easter arrangement...twelve thorny, long-stemmed stems!" laughed Phil as the clerk handed him a tissue-wrapped arrangement. "Those are for your wife?" asked Sandra. "Do you mind telling me why she wants a bouquet that looks like that?" "NO...I'm glad you asked," Phil replied. "Four years ago, my wife and I were headed to divorce. After nearly forty years, we were in a real mess, but with the Lord's grace and guidance, we trudged through problem after problem. The Lord rescued our marriage. Jenny, (the clerk), told me she kept a vase of rose stems to remind her of what she had learned from the 'thorny' times. That was good enough for me. I took home some of those stems. My wife and I decided to label each one for a specific 'problem' and give thanks for what each problem taught us."

As Phil paid the clerk, he said to Sandra, "I highly recommend the Special."

"I don't know if I can be thankful for the thorns in my life," Sandra said to the clerk. "It's all too...fresh."

"Well," the clerk replied carefully, "my experience has shown me the thorns make the roses more precious. We treasure God's providential care more during trouble than at any other time. Remember it was a crown of thorns that Jesus wore so we might know His love for us. Don't resent the thorns."

Tears rolled down Sandra's cheeks. For the first time since the accident, she loosened her grip on her resentment. "I'll take those twelve long-stemmed thorns, please," she managed to choke out.

"I hoped you would," said the clerk gently, "I'll have them ready in a minute."

"Thank you. What do I owe you?"

"Nothing. Nothing but a promise to allow God to heal your heart. The first year's arrangement is always on me."

The clerk smiled and handed a card to Sandra. "I'll attach this card to your arrangement, but maybe you would like to read it first."

It read: "*My God, I have never thanked you for my thorns. I have thanked you a thousand times for my roses, but never once for my thorns. Teach me the glory of the cross I bear; teach me the value of my thorns. Show me that I have climbed closer to you along the path of pain. Show me that, through my tears, the colors of your rainbow look much more brilliant.*"

Praise Him for the roses; thank Him for the thorns.

Prayer

Have you ever been in a group discussion where someone is talking about how much they love Jesus? How Jesus is everything and they live for Him? Then, another in the group shares her story of how bad everything is and how unfair life is, yet she lives for Jesus. Another tells her story of tragedy, through tears, but remarks about how much she loves God. I have to tell you, years ago while sitting in a Bible study, although believing in God and hearing these stories, I was thinking I am not so sure I want to be in the "followers" club. It doesn't sound like much fun to me. Also, how can you possibly be that much in love with someone you don't see, and really don't know? You may know *about* Him, but don't *know* Him.

So, I prayed for a thirst for God. I prayed to have a love for Jesus that so many talked about. I prayed to learn how to pray. I prayed not only to want to read His Word but also to understand His Word. I prayed for a servant's heart. I prayed to love others. I prayed for Him to show me purpose in my life. I prayed to be able and want to pray for others. Are you getting the idea? I prayed for everything. Although I am still a work in progress, God answered those prayers. That is one reason I am so passionate about Bible studies. I am a testimony to the phrase "Bible Study is not for Information but for Transformation."

Praying is basically communicating with God. It is not complicated; you don't have to have a theology degree. You don't have to pray out loud. There are many who fear they can't pray well enough, or right enough, or long enough, or with eloquence.

To develop an intimate love relationship with God, do two things: soak in His Word and pray. Talk with Him, be honest, voicing your heart and your thoughts. When you are "still" enough and quiet enough, you may hear His gentle whisper back. The gentle whisper is the prompting inside you. God is always faithful in affirming His answer in different ways, maybe hearing the answer again in a sermon, or in a song on the radio, or through another believer. You will become aware of the ways God communicates with you. You will get to know Him.

It is clear in the scriptures that Jesus was a prayer warrior. If Jesus was convinced that His own life and ministry depended upon prayer, shouldn't we set time apart in prayer with our Lord? (Luke 18:1, Luke 5:16, Mark 1:35, Mark 1:35, Luke 6:12)

Henry Blackaby writes: "Prayer is not for the purpose of getting God to help us...but for getting us in line with what God is about to do. Prayer is God's invitation to enter His throne room so He can lay *His agenda* over our hearts."

The scriptures tell us Jesus was in the habit of meeting with His Father in the early morning hours. Does this mean that you have to pray *in the morning*? No. He longs to hear from you anytime, all the time. But as you get thirstier for Him, you may find you love to meet with the Creator of the universe who has Words of Life, as well as daily guidance for you, first thing in the morning. This will become a source of joy, strength, and hope. This prayer time will prepare you for what you will face that day. All I am saying is this: you don't tune up the instrument *after* the concert is over.

You are full of negative emotions, disappointment, drowning in discouragement, pray for God to release you of these.

"Pray for your thoughts to be His thoughts" (Isaiah 55:8).

"Pray to think about whatever is true, noble, right, pure, lovely, admirable" (Philippians 4:8).

Philippians 4:6 reminds us to pray often. *"Do not be anxious about anything, but in everything, by prayer and petition, with thanksgiving, present your requests to God."*

Press On

I competed in two different sports at the professional level. While playing in a tournament I had a really bad day (actually to the point of embarrassment and humiliation). I had to keep playing, I couldn't quit, I had to finish the game, to press on.

God never promised every day to be "diamonds"—some days are "stones." Some days just getting out of bed IS the victory. In Philippians 3:12-14, Paul is giving a pep talk to the Christians at Philippi. He is explaining his goal is to know Christ, to be like Christ, and to be all that Christ intends for him to be. This goal consumes all of Paul's energy and should ours as well. We should stay away from anything which is harmful and be aware of what distracts us from being effective Christians. The question we need to ask ourselves is where are we spending our time daily? Do our activities strengthen us for the race or drain us and hold us back?

"I don't mean to say that I have already achieved these things or that I have already reached perfection. But I press on to possess that perfection for which Christ Jesus first possessed me. No, dear brothers and sisters, I have not achieved it, but I focus on this one thing: Forgetting the past and looking forward to what lies ahead, I press on to reach the end of the race and receive the heavenly prize for which God, through Christ Jesus, is calling us" (Philippians 3:12-14 NLT).

I am so thankful God ministers to us in so many different ways. One example is music. It ministers to my soul. Words with a melody behind it can be healing, encouraging, and sometimes just enough light for the step I am on.

The lyrics to the song "Press On" by Selah ©2001, are so encouraging to me. I recommend listening to this song; it can be a drink of water to your thirsty soul. You can find it at http://www.rhapsody.com/selah/press-on.
Let the words from James 1:12 (NLT) saturate your soul and Press On!

"God blesses those who patiently endure testing and temptation. Afterward they will receive the crown of life that God has promised to those who love Him."

Warrior Weapon

As Broken Warriors we will Praise our God, Pray to our God, and Press On toward the goal of being all God intends for us to be.

Preparing For Battle
❧❧❧

Write three scriptures to encourage you not to be discouraged.

_____

_____

_____

Read Romans 8:28 in three different translations and record all three.

_____

_____

_____

What do you think the worse thing was Hannah had to deal with?

_____

_____

_____

1. What can you relate to in this story of Hannah?

    _____

    _____

    _____

2. What promise will you take away from the story of Hannah?

_____

_____

_____

3. Hannah vowed to dedicate her first born to the Lord. What aspect of your life do you need to dedicate to God?

_____

_____

_____

    a. Children

    b. Marriage

    c. Possessions

    d. Job

    e. Future

    f. Other_____

Jesus said in Matthew 7:7, "*Ask and it will be given to you, seek and you will find; knock and the door will be opened to you.*"

Knocking on God's door means taking action, making yourself available to Him. It is one thing to know what to do; it is another to do it. Like Hannah, for those who choose to obey, a special reward awaits them. Something to think about: You can't just read the label on the medicine bottle; you have to take the pills for it to be effective.

Actions

Purchase a journal and label it "Praise Journal." Commit to writing a *praise* every day to the Lord.   I have found this extremely helpful and necessary.

To order a "Praise Journal" with explanations and starters, go to www.choosetosoar.net or call 214.563.5908

Make a schedule to pray and praise every day. If you have to write this on your schedule just like if it was a dentist appointment that is okay, especially at first to cultivate the habit. It won't be long before this "to do" item makes it on the "must do and want to" list.

Start a notebook with only encouragement verses written. Look up James 1:12 in three different translations and write these in your encouragement book.

If music lifts your soul, make a compilation of uplifting songs and write the lyrics in your encouragement book also.

Weapons of Truth

Memorize:

"*The LORD himself goes before you and will be with you;*

He will never leave you nor forsake you. Do not be afraid;

do not be discouraged" (Deuteronomy 31:8).

Digging Deeper

Re-read 1 Samuel 1: 1-28. As you read, read it out loud. Observe what is going on in these verses. Try to write down at least 20 questions you come up with about this passage, don't worry about the answers, just questions.

_____

_____

_____

_____

In Chapter 1 of Samuel 2:1-10, Hannah's Prayer is often compared to another prayer. Whose? And Why?

_____

_____

_____

Explain Hannah's story and the three Ps to someone else. Typically you will learn more by trying to explain to someone else.

Read Philippians 3:12-21.

What is the prize Paul is talking about?

_____

_____

_____

What does it mean to live as enemies of Christ (verse 18)

_____

_____

_____

What will you do differently daily starting immediately to press on toward the goal? Write this action so you will see it daily.

_____

_____

_____

Further Reading
Daily Experience with God by Andrew Murray

Chapter 3
ฝฝฝ

Kingdom Wardrobe

"Therefore, put on every piece of God's armor so you will be able to resist the enemy in the time of evil. Then after the battle you will still be standing firm" (Ephesians 6:13 NLT).

Driving 45 minutes one way to soccer practice and games three times a week is common in my household. One day in particular practice was canceled. However, I was not notified in time so I drove all the way to the fields to find no one there. As I was driving the 45 minutes back home, I began to process how I was not notified in time and how disrespectful this was to me. This cost me in not only gas but also nearly two hours of my time, which I value greatly. To add to the fire, this same exact scenario happened to me about 6 weeks before.

By the time I got home, I was all fired up and not in a good way. Because I was in such a rage, I couldn't think straight. Now I know you shouldn't get this mad over something this small, but it happens, or should I say, I let it happen. Anyway, the first thing I did when I got home was fire off an email not only to the manager, but to the whole team. As soon as I hit "send" on the computer, the battle was over. It was like an 'out of body' experience. I realized what I had done and that I had been "had" by the enemy. I won't go into the details or the hurtful words that were said after this poisoned note was sent, but I can tell you I felt like a jigsaw puzzle with a couple of pieces gone. I pray this chapter will equip you and help prevent something like this happening to you.

Stop the Digging

This next statement may be a little strong but true: DO NOT get complacent with the enemy of God! We are in a constant battle with Satan. Whatever glorifies God angers the enemy. As Christians, we are under persecution all the time. I know this is not what you wanted to hear—me neither. Jesus tells us we should expect opposition and persecution from the world. However, He also gives us many promises and hope. In John 16, He tells us not to lose hope the victory is His. He *has overcome the world*. Paul reminds us in Romans: *If God is for us, who can be against us?*

Spiritual warfare is real and our enemy is real. Satan is very sneaky and a master of disguises; so if you think you will recognize him when you see him, you are wrong. I used to think as I matured in my walk with the Lord I would get better at recognizing the enemy, but *I* was wrong. Just think about where he spends his time. I don't think Satan spends a lot of time focused on the bad guys. I think he is focused on the church, the un-alert Christians, the Christians moving others towards God. Where was Satan the

night Jesus was betrayed? He was not with the bad guys, the
Pharisees; Satan was in the Upper Room, in Judas, betraying Jesus.

Paul, the author of Ephesians, writes specifically in Chapter
6:10-20 about the enemy. I believe that since Paul was chained to a
Roman soldier, and these soldiers were common in that day, he
used their equipment to illustrate God's weapons available to us. As
soon as you realize, "the Christian life is a battleground, not a
playground," as Warren Wiersbe writes, then the more joy you will
experience. And because of the Cross, Christ overcame the world
(John 16:33). Christ is the victor. Therefore, as believers, we do not
fight *for* victory but rather *from* victory. And what Paul tells us in
this passage is, if we apply God's truths, we will walk in victory also.

Understanding the way Satan works will help us with our
suffering. One way Satan attacks, which seems most effective on
women, is to target our emotions, our hearts. Our hearts are the
door to our emotions and our self-worth. Nothing pleases the
enemy more then when we "dig our own pit." Some of us have dug
a beautiful pit, spent time decorating it, getting things in j-u-s-t the
right place, waiting for company, and yet no one ever knocks on the
door of our pit, except ourselves.

I have searched scriptures to find how effective such a pit can
be, or if there is a sense of joy and peace in having your own pit. I'm
still looking. Self-pity is a destructive, worthless, downright
U-G-L-Y place. Don't go there; don't even pick up the shovel. *Stop*

digging. I say we get T-shirts made with that slogan; better yet, a tattoo! (Just kidding, Mom)

Attacking our hearts is one of Satan's favorite tactical moves. Just like the wars that have been fought in our lifetime, there must be strategies. You must know who the enemy is, where he is, and what he can do. Otherwise, you will be defeated.

Two actions we can put into place to be prepared for the attacks are:

Be Aware!

Be Alert!

(Matthew 4:3, John 8:44, 1 Peter 5:8, Genesis 3:1, 2 Corinthians 11:13-15, 2 Corinthians. 4:4)

God has given us the Bible to instruct us about the enemy and how to defeat him and not be caught off guard.

As you are being aware and alert, pay attention to your thoughts. Are you thinking the whole world is against you? I know, life isn't fair to you because...but we could all say the same thing. Yes, trials happen, life is not fair! Our enemy wants us to really dwell on these things. Some of our suffering is from our own choices and some because we have been the victim of someone else's poor choices. God does redeem and forgive us and knows strength of our flesh. However, don't you love the fact that God is a God of second chances? Actually, He is the God of many chances. I am so thankful He has patience with me and forgives me. But our enemy looks for any window slightly open to our mind and heart to get his foot in and continue with his lies and deceitful ways.

Let's understand something about our enemy, Satan. He is limited in his knowledge and activity, unlike God. Satan uses his own army to help with his evil. Remember Satan wanted to be like God, and thought he could be, so God casted him out of heaven. I know this may sound hokey, and is hard to understand, but just trust the scriptures. This is what Paul is talking about in Ephesians 6:12. Revelation 12:4 and Daniel 10:13-20 allude to angels falling with Satan and the struggles against God's angels for control of nations. In other words, as Wiersbe puts it, a spiritual battle is going on in this world, in the sphere of "the heavenlies," and you and I are a part of this battle.

> *"Know that our battle is not against human beings, it is against spiritual powers. So we are wasting our time fighting people when we ought to be fighting the devil who* seeks *to control people and make them oppose the work of God"* (Warren Wiersbe).

Have you ever heard the phrase, "Hurting people hurt people"? Satan is behind it all. Please don't stop reading. If this tripped your "weird meter", it is okay. Believe me, there are some hard things to understand in the Bible and you will never understand it all, at least not while here on this planet. But have faith, trust God with the basics of His love and mercy, stay teachable. I promise He will bring light and understanding to you when you are ready to receive it.

Throughout scriptures, there are warnings of Satan's power... Use these verses to help you stay aware and alert and help you recognize the enemy.

"The thief comes only to steal and kill and destroy; I have come that they may have life, and have it to the full" (John 10:10).

"And no wonder, for Satan himself masquerades as an angel of light" (2 Corinthians 11:14).

"Be self-controlled and alert. Your enemy, the devil, prowls around like a roaring lion looking for someone to devour" (1 Peter 5:8).

"For you are the children of your father, the devil, and you love to do the evil things he does. He was a murderer from the beginning. He has always hated the truth, because there is no truth in him. When he lies, it is consistent with his character; for he is a liar and the father of lies" (John 8:44 NLT).

What to Wear

Be encouraged Broken Warriors, that we have hope, we have guidance, promises and protection. We have a Kingdom Wardrobe. The wardrobe may not have a lot of bling, but with some cute earrings, it will be perfect.

The wardrobe is worn for our protection as we battle life. The wardrobe is listed in Ephesians 6:13-17. These verses are listing the pieces of the Armor of God, *Kingdom Wardrobe.* As I attempt to describe and explain each piece, one thing to keep in mind is this armor is meant to be worn as a complete outfit. You wouldn't wear your favorite jeans and blouse without the right belt, earrings and shoes, would you? It's the same with the armor-it is meant to be worn all together. Trust me. Many times I wore the armor piecemeal and I have the wounds to show for it. Yet another reason for the title, "Broken Warrior".

"Therefore, put on every piece of God's armor so you will be able to resist the enemy in the time of evil. Then after the battle you will still be standing firm. Stand your ground, putting on the belt of truth and the body armor of God's righteousness. For shoes, put on the peace that comes from the Good News so that you will be fully prepared. In addition to all of these, hold up the shield of faith to stop the fiery arrows of the devil. Put on salvation as your helmet,

and take the sword of the Spirit, which is the word of God"
(Ephesians 6:13-17 NLT)

The equipment consists of the following items:

      Belt of Truth

      Breastplate of Righteousness

      Shoes of the Gospel

      Shield of Faith

      Helmet of Salvation

      Sword of the Spirit

Paul, the Author of Ephesians, compares each of these character traits to a part of a Roman soldier's armor. This is the order they are given in scripture. However, it might help you remember the pieces better if we put them "on" in order of how we get dressed. Let's start with the Breastplate of Righteousness.

Breastplate of Righteousness

In choosing my outfit for the day, I usually start with picking what blouse I want to wear. Think of your shirt as the Breastplate of Righteousness. Paul describes to the Ephesians in verse 14, a piece of armor called the Breastplate of Righteousness. This piece of armor fits over and around the Roman soldier's midsection. Typically, it was made of metal and bronzed with a reddish color to intimidate the opposing enemy.

The function of the breastplate is to protect the soldier's vital organs, the heart, and lungs. You could have injury to an arm or leg or even your head and even though impaired, you would still function. BUT, have a sword plunged in your heart, and you are finished!

This gives new meaning to Proverbs 4:23:

"Above all else, guard your heart, for it is the wellspring of life."

Satan loves to attack our hearts, which my Bible commentary explains is the seat of our emotions, our self-worth, and trust. God knows about our heart, He created it. God has provided this piece of armor for our protection and ensures His approval and love for us (righteousness).

As Christians, we are given God's righteousness. We should ask ourselves if we are living a godly life in the power of the Spirit. Or are we making it easier for our enemy to defeat us?

By strapping on this breastplate, not only are we covering ourselves with God's promises of protection, but we also stop focusing on what the world and the enemy has told us. Start focusing on God and become preoccupied with obedience to Him; this, my friend, overwhelms the enemy every time.

> *The righteousness of Christ in you is what matters — not your shortcomings and failures.*

Warrior Weapon

Strap on the Breastplate of Righteousness daily!

Belt of Truth

The next piece—as much as I want it to be a cute, fashionable, blingy belt—must be a strong belt, one that can be strapped on tight. This Belt of Truth has to be tight to hold the other armor together, and the sword. The Belt of Truth is what fights Satan's lies that he puts in our minds. The tricky part is Satan can make his lies sound like truth. Look what he did to Eve. YIKES!

Beware; our enemy knows scripture also, just not that well. He manipulates it to make it seem like truth. This is very harmful to the kingdom. Therefore, as Broken Warriors how do we put on this Belt of Truth tight. It means we must not only know the truth, we need to **practice** the truth. How many lives have been ruined or halted because of Satan's lies? Eve followed the enemy progression (Genesis 3).

> She Listened to a Lie,
>
> She Dwelled on the Lie,
>
> She Believed in the Lie
>
> She Acted on the Lie,
>
> Result---the fall of man!

In Psalm 32, King David is talking about his behavior from a lie planted about his sin with Bathsheba. I don't think David had the Belt of Truth on, but he did confess, as you will see when you read that Psalm.

As a fellow Broken Warrior, let me ask you some questions:

1. What are some of the destructive lies Satan has planted in you?
2. Have you ever allowed someone else's opinion of you to become the centerpiece of your existence?
3. What has been the result of believing those lies?
4. What lies have you unwittingly planted in the lives of your own children?

There are no harmless lies. Eve's first mistake wasn't eating the fruit. Her first mistake was listening to the serpent. Eve might have benefitted from what we have often said in my household when we are in the company of negative influences: "Remove yourself from the situation."

So how do we recognize our crafty enemy's lies?

Anytime we receive input that is not consistent with the Word of God we can be sure Satan is trying to deceive and destroy us. What we read or hear may sound right, it may feel right, and you want to believe it is right, BUT if it is contrary to the Word of God, it is not right!

God's truth is more powerful than our enemy's lies (1 Peter 5:8, James 4:7, 1 John 4:4).

Let's not let Satan's lies enter our minds. A life controlled by the Truth can defeat him.

Warrior Weapon

Put on and tighten the Belt of Truth daily!

Shoes of the Gospel

I can really relate to this piece of armor. Between my daughter, and me it is embarrassing how many pairs of shoes we have. You might say we have a shoe fetish. Anyway, I am not so sure we are thinking the same as Paul about this subject. Again using the equipment of the Roman Soldier as an illustration, Paul tells us to be prepared to spread the Gospel, the good news.

The Soldiers wore sandals with a type of cleat in the sole to give them better footing for the battle. A stability of sorts, much like wearing golf shoes when playing golf so you can stand firm. Go back and read, verse 10-14 and see how many times Paul uses the word "stand." If we are going to "stand" and "withstand," then we need the Shoes of the Gospel.

These shoes are often referred to as the Gospel of Peace. Because God has given us peace that comes from the Gospel, we need not fear our enemy. We must also be at peace with each other.

The scripture reads..."and with your feet fitted with the readiness..." This means to be prepared and willing to go and share the Gospel of Peace. For those who think this means standing on the street corner, holding a sign with "John 3:16" printed in bold letters and using a megaphone to shout to everyone, "The end is near, do you know Jesus?"— you can breathe a sigh of relief. What this means is being willing to tell others what God has done in your life, and being willing to ask someone you just met how you can pray for them. It means planting seeds about God and His saving grace and love to those you live with, work with, and socialize with. Putting on these shoes means being prepared if someone says something derogatory about your God and His ways or asking about His love.

> *"Always be prepared to give an answer to everyone who asks you to give the reason for the hope that you have"*
> (1 Peter 3:15).

One more thing: I didn't say these shoes were necessarily comfortable. We are to be willing to move out of our comfort zone and share the Gospel, to talk about the tough stuff. Go after those on whom Satan has a stronghold. This type of "walk the talk" defeats Satan every time.

> *Real peace is surrendering to Christ, who is the Prince of Peace.*

As a Broken Warrior, ask yourself if you are prepared for questions about the Gospel? Are you ready to share the Gospel? Are you at peace with God and others? Are you at peace with yourself?

Maybe it is time to take off the slippery flip-flops and put on the stable Shoes of the Gospel.

Warrior Weapon

Put on the Shoes of the Gospel daily!

Helmet of Salvation

After I get dressed, I usually check my hair one last time. Do I need to brush it again, put more products in to make it just right or just turn upside down, and use my fingers to fluff? These are major decisions, right? Well according to Paul "who I am thinking was not a hairdresser" tells us we need the Helmet of Salvation to protect our minds from Satan's attacks. The helmet is to protect our thought life.

Satan wants us to doubt God and His plan for us, to question His love and our salvation. I am thinking Eve needed a helmet instead of a piece of fruit. We are to have the mind of Christ. When we let God control our mind, Satan cannot lead the believer astray. Have you ever been led astray? Yeah, me too. I was too worried about my hair and not my mind.

> *"But I am afraid that just as Eve was deceived by the serpent's cunning, your minds may somehow be led astray from your sincere and pure devotion to Christ"* (2 Corinthians 11:3).

How do we avoid these attacks to the mind? Soak up what scripture tells us.

> *"The weapons we fight with are not the weapons of the world. On the contrary, they have divine power to demolish strongholds. We demolish arguments and every pretension that sets itself up against the knowledge of God, and we take captive every thought to make it obedient to Christ"* (2 Corinthians 10:4-5).

> *"The mind of a sinful man is death. But the mind controlled by the Spirit is life and peace"* (Romans 8:6).

"Do not conform any longer to the pattern of this world, but be transformed by the renewing of your mind. Then you will be able to test and approve what God's will is—his good, pleasing and perfect will" (Romans 12:2).

"Set your minds on things above, not on earthly things" (Colossians 3:2).

"The end of all things is near. Therefore be clear minded and self-controlled so that you can pray" (1 Peter 4:7).

"Finally, brothers, whatever is true, whatever is noble, whatever is right, whatever is pure, whatever is lovely, whatever is admirable—if anything is excellent or praiseworthy—think about such things" (Philippians 4:8).

"Those who are spiritual can evaluate all things, but they themselves cannot be evaluated by others. For, 'Who can know the LORD's thoughts? Who knows enough to teach him?'But we understand these things, for we have the mind of Christ" (1 Corinthians 2:15-16).

Psalm 1:1-3 tells us to meditate on His Word day and night. Reading His Word keeps our minds thinking and moving in the right direction, protecting us from the kind of thinking that is harmful to ourselves and others.

> *"At all times, keep straight in your mind who you are. You are a child of God. Christ has saved you from sin and death. These truths will guard your mind."*   (Daily Strength for the Battle)

Warrior Weapon

Put on the Helmet of Salvation daily!

Shield of Faith

Now I am dressed and ready. As I start to leave, I pick up my purse, which I am calling the Shield of Faith. The soldier's shield was large, made of wood but covered in very tough leather. The soldier could hold it in front of him or around him to protect himself from spears and arrows. The scripture calls them "fiery darts." The reason they call them "fiery darts" is because arrows were dipped into a substance that you could ignite before they were shot at the enemy. This is exactly what Satan does to us. He shoots these darts into our minds and hearts. These darts are hateful thoughts and doubts. The list is long but all the darts create a burning desire for sin. Our mission tag line for our ministry,

Choose to Soar, is "Igniting Faith...Changing Lives." I am thinking Satan's line is "igniting sin...destroying lives."

The soldier's shield was often soaked in water to extinguish the burning arrows shot at him. Our Shield of Faith will extinguish our enemy's "fiery darts." What does that look like, practically speaking? It means having faith in God, walking in faith daily, and trusting Him.

*Trusting in God's Word as truth
*Trusting God's provision
*Trusting God will protect us from the evil one
*Believing through faith we have Christ's authority over evil powers

Did you ever watch Star Trek? I did and my husband occasionally still does. But don't call him a trekky, okay, just " live long and prosper." Anyway, the starship Enterprise was equipped with electromagnetic shields. When in battle they could raise their shields and this protected the whole ship from shots fired from the enemy. However, there were many shows where the ship lost power, shields were not at a 100%, and then their enemy would do great damage to this weakened vessel. Hmmm, reminds me of someone; does it you? You see, when we start believing Satan's lies, entertaining thoughts we know are not from God, and failing to block them with the Shield of Faith, we do great damage to God's weakened vessel."

I pick up my purse and take it with me everywhere. Let's think the same way about the Shield of Faith. I know we take our purse with us when we leave the house, but what if we carried it around with us in our home. Now there's a thought. Yes, those "fiery darts" can be shot at us maybe more so in our own home. If you don't think Satan uses our kids and spouse to shoot fiery darts, think again. As I said, the devil is a master of disguises. I am thinking I will just put the armor on and never take it off. Not sure how well that will go over with the husband, but I don't think Satan ever sleeps.

Warrior Weapon

Pick up the Shield of Faith daily!

Sword of the Spirit

There is something I know you don't leave home without making sure you have it with you. I make sure I have it *with me* when I am at home, at a restaurant, at a soccer game, even while working out. One time, I took this with me on a kayak. I feel like something is missing if I don't have it with me.

Okay, enough of the riddle. What is it?

Your cell phone! Am I right? We go into a small panic if we don't know where it is. Heaven forbid we go anywhere without our cell phone.

I wonder how many of us feel that way about God's Word. I mean, do you go to watch your kid's or grandkid's soccer game and have scriptures running through your head? This would really help when the game starts heating up and the parents are out of control. Or how about when you are at a restaurant eating with friends? Do certain verses or passages pop in your mind? Do you know enough scripture for it to pop in your mind? Yikes. I know that one hurt.

The Sword of the Spirit is the only offensive weapon God provides us. The Roman soldier wore his sword on his belt (Belt of Truth) and the sword is for fighting close-up. The Word is compared to a sword because "it is living and sharper than any double-edged sword" (Hebrews 4:12).

A real sword will pierce the body, will hurt, and kill. But the Word of God pierces the heart, *to heal and give life*. Warren Weirsbe writes, "The more you use a physical sword, the duller it becomes, but using God's Word only makes it sharper in our lives."

The soldier had to practice using the sword to get good and comfortable for when the battle started. We are the same. We must practice using God's Word. This means memorizing scripture and reading His Word to get understanding and insight into the power and love of God.

Satan hates God's Word. Jesus used nothing but the Word to defeat Satan's temptations in the desert (Luke 4:1-13). This is crucial: we had better know the Word of God because Satan does too. Satan just knows the Word enough to confuse us and to make us doubt. This is why we must know scriptures so we can detect Satan's lies and know what truth is.

Warrior Weapon

Pick up the Sword of the Spirit daily!

Whole Armor of God

As Broken Warriors, we will get fully dressed every day with the armor of God. Think about this action as being *clothed in Jesus.*

"Rather, clothe yourselves with the Lord Jesus Christ, and do not think about how to gratify the desires of the sinful nature" (Romans 13:14).

Each piece has tremendous significance. God has given us these tools to use as His Warriors. Put on the armor and trust God for the victory. One more note worth mentioning to help us understand the importance of the armor, even for the seasoned Christian, is found in 2 Samuel Chapter 11. The writer tells us the story of King David. David's life took a very wrong turn, even after fighting in many battles, defeating great enemies, building a nation, and restoring Israel. He commits adultery, then murder, and then loses the child conceived during the affair. When David had his armor on in battle on the battlefield, he was victorious. The minute he took off the armor and returned home, he suffered great damage. This should be a reminder that we are always in the enemy's bulls-eye and Satan is just waiting and watching for us to put our armor down so he can attack us when defenseless.

There is a song by the Christian music group, Casting Crowns, titled "The Voice of Truth." Listen to the lyrics of this song, and especially the chorus, for encouragement for us Broken Warriors.
http://www.youtube.com/watch?v=FuH1faTC22E&feature=related

Warrior Weapon

Broken Warriors choose to listen and believe the voice of Truth.

Preparing for Battle
෨෨෨

Record the following scriptures: Matthew 4:3, John 8:44,
1 Peter 5:8, Genesis 3:1, 2 Corinthians 4:4, Romans 13:12

How would you use these scriptures to explain our enemy to someone?

_____

_____

_____

What is significant about each piece of armor?

_____

_____

_____

Which piece(s) do you regularly forget to wear?

_____

_____

_____

a. How will you remember to put on that particular piece?_____

_____

_____

What will you do to ensure you have the whole armor on daily?

_____

_____

_____

b. Write down your plan and/or prayer and put it where you can see it daily.

_____

_____

_____

What lie has Satan planted in you that you re-play over in your mind?

_____

_____

_____

    c. Write a scripture (Voice of Truth) that tells you otherwise.

_____

_____

_____

Weapons of Truth

Memorize:

"*Therefore, put on every piece of God's armor so you will be able to resist the enemy in the time of evil. Then after the battle you will still be standing firm*" (Ephesians 6:13NLT).

Digging Deeper

What other verses reference spiritual weapons?

_____

_____

_____

Read Ephesians 6:18-20

What is Paul asking for?_____

What does prayer enable us to do with the armor?

_____

_____

_____

What does Paul mean by "making known the mystery of the gospel?"

_____

_____

_____

How would you explain verse 18 to someone?

_____

_____

_____

What does it mean to pray in the Spirit?

_____

_____

_____

How do you stay alert and *always* keep praying?

_____

_____

_____

Who are the saints he is referencing?

_____

_____

_____

Chapter 4
❧❧❧

Please Sir, Could I Have Some More?

"...I do believe; help me overcome my unbelief" (Mark 9:24).

How did you get to work, church, or anywhere today? You probably drove some sort of vehicle. My question to you is this: did you have faith that as you were traveling on the road at 60+ miles per hour that the approaching cars would stay on their side of the road?

My faith is being tested because my daughter just received her driver's permit. This will also increase your prayer life. Anyway, talk about having faith! Now I am praying she will stay on *her side* of the road.

Our faith is often tested and stretched. I pray this chapter brings you to a deeper understanding of your faith and helps increase your faith as well.

Defining Faith

Let's say there is a fire in the second story of a house. There is a child at the window of a room next to the fire. The only way out in time for the child is to jump into a neighbor's arms that arrived at the scene first. The man on the ground is shouting to the child, "Drop into my arms. Don't be afraid. I'll catch you."

It is one part of faith for the child to know the man is there. It is another part of faith to believe the man is strong and able to catch him. However, the *essence* of faith lies in the child dropping down into the man's arms.

Developing Faith

George Mueller, a great man of faith, once said, "God delights to increase the faith of His children. Trials, obstacles, difficulties, and sometimes defeats, are the very food of faith."

Lacking Faith

A man was walking along a narrow path, not paying much attention to where he was going. Suddenly he slipped over the edge of a cliff. As he fell, he grabbed a branch growing from the side of the cliff. Realizing he could not hang on for long, he called for help.

Man: Is anybody up there?

Voice: Yes, I'm here!

Man: Who?

Voice: The Lord.

Man: Lord, help me!

Voice: Do you trust me?

Man: I trust you completely, Lord.

Voice: Good. Let go of the branch.

Man: What???

Voice: I said, Let go of the branch.

Man: (after a long pause) is anybody else up there?

This story reminds me of the story in the Bible from Mark 9:14-29.

To summarize; a man brings his demon-possessed child to the disciples for them to drive out the evil spirit. The disciples had been given the authority by Jesus to heal, but they couldn't heal this boy. The embarrassed disciples (whom I'm sure were probably resting on their past successes and got a little too big for their robes) were probably provoked by the educated teachers of the law who were in the crowd, and they started arguing. Jesus asks, "What are you arguing with them about?" The father of the boy explains why he is there with his son. Then Jesus speaks out to them, not just the disciples but all those around saying with a likely disappointed tone, "O unbelieving generation, how long shall I stay with you? How long shall I put up with you? Bring the boy to me." Jesus then asks the boy's father "How long he had been like this?"

Listen to how the father replies to the question, "From childhood. It has often thrown him into fire or water to kill him. *But if you can do anything*, take pity on us and help us."

What! Are you kidding? Did he just ask Jesus if he could do anything? I love the way Jesus replies: "If you can?" Notice the question mark. This is a rhetorical question. Then Jesus, responds with what I think is a calm, confident answer, "Everything is possible for him who believes."

Because of the failure of the disciples, and the father apparently put his faith in them and they failed him, he was not even sure at this point if Jesus could help. Maybe the reason for his next response.

> *Immediately the boy's father exclaimed, "I do believe; help me overcome my unbelief!"* (Mark 9:24).

Notice the scriptures want you to see and feel the anxiousness of the situation by telling us the father exclaimed "*immediately,* I do believe." Then following the fathers exclamation of belief, he pauses, then declares his true need, "*help me overcome my unbelief!*"

Okay, which is it: does he believe or doesn't he? Does this remind you of yourself? Of course, it is easy to have faith when we see God doing things we have asked for. We shout, "I believe." "Yeah God." But the minute things don't line up with our plans and there is no way we can see how our circumstances can be used for good, we start to question, we start to limit God, and we start to ask *if* He can.

We tend to be like the boy's father and first put our faith in others; then, when they don't come through, we then turn to God. If we trust God completely and our faith is in Him, shouldn't we go to

Him first? In addition, we shouldn't be disappointed, no matter the outcome.

This scripture confirms we must have faith.

"And without faith it is impossible to please God, because anyone who comes to Him must believe that He exists and that He rewards those who earnestly seek Him"
(Hebrews 11:6).

Warrior Weapon

Stop asking God "If He can" and start praying for Him to help me with my unbelief!

Object of Faith

No one believes in nothing. Everyone has faith. The difference is the object of our faith. The degree of faith that one places in a given object is directly proportional to one's knowledge of the object.

I find it interesting while in a plane, sitting still on the ground, your seat belt must be fastened, but when traveling at 500 mph at 35,000 feet, you don't have to? Do you have more faith at 35,000 feet?

I know the more I learn about the Lord, the more faith I place in Him. The power of faith rests in the reliability of its object.

Where are you on the faith meter? Perhaps you are in a "faith developing life storm" right now. Do you relate to the man who fell off the cliff and is barely hanging on, and still won't let God come to the rescue? In what are you putting your faith? Is your limitation of faith controlling your life?

"Forsaking all, I take Him."
Henrietta Mears

Limiting Faith

Are we afraid to risk disappointment with God, so we limit Him? Do you believe the way we live is a consequence of the size of our God? We make Him small. Are we not convinced we are absolutely safe in the arms of a fully competent, all-knowing ever-present God?

Do we live in a constant state of fear and anxiety because we think everything depends on us? Do we become slaves to what others think of us? We have too little faith.

My story of limiting faith is light, but has a very valid point. This happened while I was just finishing this chapter. I was lying down on the couch because of a migraine headache. As I was in a light sleep with "Pumpkin," the cat, lying on my legs and "Luke," the dog, lying on the floor next to me, something hit the kitchen window. The cat hunched up, I sprung up and the dog sat up on alert. What in the world was that? My first thought was maybe a kid kicked a soccer ball into the window, but it was the middle of the day so no kids were home. I didn't hear any more noise after the hit against the window so I ruled out someone trying to break in. My next thought was perhaps a bird flew into the window. I walked to the kitchen window, slowly twirled the blinds open, afraid of what I might see. There he was, a bird lying flat on the ground gasping for life. It was pitiful, he laid there with his little beak opening, and shutting; I could tell he was struggling to breathe. His eyes wide open but full of panic, and of course I thought he was looking at me to do something. I didn't know what to do. I couldn't stand to watch him suffer like that, so I twirled the blinds back shut and begin to pray for the bird. (This is where my daughter and husband started laughing at me as I told them the story.) Anyway, I prayed, "God, I know you watch over everything, go ahead, take the bird's life, I can't stand to see him suffer." It wasn't long, I took another look out the window, and there he laid, beak not moving, eyes closed. He had gone to birdie heaven.

I went about my business, and about an hour later, I was going to take out the trash and I knew I had better get the dead bird off the porch. I went to the window, twirled the blinds open, and the bird was gone. My first thought was I was going to go in the back yard and find him hobbling on one leg and flapping with one wing. Then what would I do? As I searched the back yard, he was nowhere to be found. Where did he go? Could a cat have gotten him? No, because my cat is the only cat around and he is inside. A dog couldn't have gotten through our wrought-iron fence. Where is he? Then I got excited. The Lord had resurrected the bird! Hallelujah!

At first, that story tickled my funny bone. Then I heard this inner voice saying, "Wow, Tanya, you just limited your faith again." You know, I most certainly did. I never once thought about praying for the bird to live. I didn't see how it was possible for the bird to live, so of course I didn't pray any other way except what I thought was in the realm of possibilities.

How many times a day do we limit God? Why do we insist on making Him small? We don't seem to ask God for things bigger than we are. God commands us to ask for what we need.

> *"Have faith in God," Jesus answered. "I tell you the truth, if anyone says to this mountain, 'Go, throw yourself into the sea,' and does not doubt in his heart but believes that what he says will happen, it will be done for him. Therefore I tell you, whatever you ask for in prayer, believe that you have received it, and it will be yours"*   (Mark 11:22-24).

"In that day you will no longer ask me anything. I tell you the truth, my Father will give you whatever you ask in my name. Until now you have not asked for anything in my name. Ask and you will receive, and your joy will be complete" (John 16:23-24).

"Ask and it will be given to you; seek and you will find; knock and the door will be opened to you. For everyone who asks receives; he who seeks finds; and to him who knocks, the door will be opened" (Matthew 7:7-8).

> *Faith is not a "feeling," it is our response to what God has revealed in His Word.*

Warrior Weapon

Stop Limiting God!

Childlike Faith

"He called a little child and had him stand among them. And he said: 'I tell you the truth, unless you change and become like little children, you will never enter the kingdom of

heaven. Therefore, whoever humbles himself like this child is the greatest in the kingdom of heaven" (Matthew 18:2-4).

When I was a child, the excitement I had during December with Christmas approaching was like no other. The parties at school, the shopping, and decorating to be done, kept me in a constant "in awe" mode. And of course, the anxiousness of opening presents on December 25 was almost more than I could stand.

I believe Jesus was trying to tell us to approach Him with this same excitement, this same kind of wonder. Jesus wants us humbled. Not looking inward at ourselves, or trying to impress others. We shouldn't think we have to feel a certain way to approach Him or even have complete understanding. He wants us to have that childlike faith, to just run to His open arms and enjoy the gift of His love, His presence (presents). Christmas morn all the time.

In New Testament days, a child was considered of no importance, receiving no attention or favor. So imagine the disciples' confusion when Jesus told them to become like little children. Don't let sophistication stand in the way of having a childlike faith in Jesus.

Warrior Weapon

Approach God with excitement and the humbleness of a child!

Increasing Faith

The title of this chapter is "Please Sir, Could I Have Some More." My daughter, Taylor and I say this phrase often, taken from the movie "Scrooge" where poor crippled Tiny Tim asks his father for another serving at dinner. We try to emulate the phrase by using a British accent and bending over slightly: "Please suh, coud I ave sum more?"

Tiny Tim was asking for more food. Taylor and I use that phrase also when we want more goodies, and I believe the disciples could have used this phrase when they asked Jesus for more faith.

Look at Luke 17:5, the disciples' statement to Jesus to "increase their faith" seems an odd and random request because it comes after Jesus says to them,

> *"Watch yourselves. If your brother sins, rebuke him, and if he repents, forgive him. If he sins against you seven times in a day, and seven times comes back to you and says, 'I repent, forgive him.'*

After their request, then Jesus replies in verse 6,

> *"If you have faith as small as a mustard seed, you can say to this mulberry tree, 'Be uprooted and planted in the sea,' and it will obey you."*

I wonder if the disciples' request of "increase our faith" might have been said sarcastically. Jesus is telling them about this forgiveness they must have (verses 1-4) and in the Tanya Standard Version, the disciples said sarcastically, "Well, then you better give us some sort of power in order to forgive like that." My guess is, it was Peter who responded. Out of the Twelve (disciples), Peter was the most outspoken. I tend to be a lot like Peter, and this is definitely something I would say. Although it isn't stated here, maybe there was a pause before they responded with their genuine request of "increase our faith." Because the text says "our" faith, I think the disciples might have had a pow-wow first and then realized increased faith was necessary for such radical forgiveness.

Again, Jesus reminds them, in Luke 17:6, it is not the *amount* of faith necessary but the *right kind* of faith. The only way they could obey Jesus and do what He asks is through faith and action. Action is a major player with faith. You can't just have faith and expect all the work will get done while you sit on the couch and eat bon-bons. Jesus expects us to combine faith with action.

Warrior Weapon

Ask the Lord to increase my faith; then put wheels to it!

Feeling Faith

I don't know about you, but I know I have got myself into some real messes because of viewing life through "feelings." Does the term, PMS, mean anything to you? Well then, you know how your feelings can vary day-to-day, hour-to-hour, or in many cases, minute-by-minute.

We do need to remember faith is not a feeling. Faith means relinquishing control, and trusting God with the good and the bad. Trusting Him and believing Romans 8:28 with all your heart.

> *"And we know that in all things God works for the good of those who love Him, who have been called according to His purpose"* (*Romans 8:28*).

Don't think you won't have doubts sometimes because you will. Why is it, that in trials, faith can be ignited in some people, yet, in others destroyed?

We clearly see why we should praise God. However, when something tragic happens, we question His existence.

> "My business is not to prove to any other man that there is a God, but to find him for myself."
>
> George Macdonald, *Thomas Wingfold*

Jesus knew the disciples doubted many times. We got a glimpse of this in the scriptures we just explored. Here is what we can learn from the Twelve (disciples): they may have doubted, but they worshipped. They served, and helped each other while they doubted. In their case, however, they got to see for themselves— their doubt was put to rest. Three days after the cross, their doubts turned to belief. And so should ours. We will never understand the depth of God and if we did, He wouldn't be God.

What I am suggesting is as you trust God more, and turn over more control to Him, you will see He tends to do a much better job with your life than you can. That is not to say He will always show you why He allows things to happen or not happen, but know He loves you more than anyone else ever could. His plans are to prosper you and not harm you.

> *'For I know the plans I have for you,' declares the LORD, 'plans to prosper you and not to harm you, plans to give you hope and a future'"* (Jeremiah 29:11).

Maybe you fear the unexpected. You are not alone. However, there are many stories in the Bible of those who wanted to do things their way and it didn't turn out so well. Actually, I don't believe there is one story in the Bible of someone who did it their way and the results were great. I know I don't have to look far to see what happens when you take matters into your own hands.

Heroes of Faith

There are all kinds of Heroes. There are animated superheroes, war heroes, sandwich heroes, Guitar Hero® and many more. But the greatest list of heroes of all time had something in common: tremendous faith. In Hebrews Chapter 11, the "Hall of Faith" chapter, all the heroes introduced, have a preceding title, "By faith..." For example:

By faith Noah...
By faith Abraham...
By faith Moses...
By faith the people passed through the Red Sea...
By faith the walls of Jericho fell...
By faith the prostitute Rahab...

These are just some of the greats. And I betting at some point, each of these heroes doubted and asked God to increase their faith.

The following are two stories of present-day Heroes of Faith. The first one is set in the late 1800s, and the last one is in the late 1900s.

Horatio Spafford was a successful lawyer and business man, a dedicated and active Christian. In 1871, all of Spafford's real estate holdings were wiped out. Shortly afterwards, upon the advice of their family physician, they planned a European vacation. At the last minute, an unexpected business situation required him to remain in Chicago for a few days, so he sent his wife and four daughters ahead on the ship.

On November 22, 1873, in calm seas the ill-fated ship collided with another ship in the North Atlantic and, in only twelve minutes, it sank. Mrs. Spafford was saved, but all four daughters perished. Mrs. Spafford cabled her husband a two-word message, "Saved Alone."

Horatio immediately left by ship to be with his wife and on the high seas, near the scene of the tragedy, he wrote the words to the great hymn, "It is Well with My Soul."

A floating oar miraculously saved Mrs. Spafford. "Why her? How could she face life without her children?"

Bertha Spafford Vester, their daughter born after the tragedy at sea, has written a graphic account recalled by her mother entitled "Our Jerusalem."

In the moment of returning to consciousness, Anna lifted her soul to God in an agony of despair and Anna Spafford said it was as if a voice spoke to her, "You are spared for a purpose. You have work to do." Anna Spafford humbly dedicated her life to His service.

They move to Jerusalem to establish the American Colony. Because of their circumstances, untold thousands of Jews and Arabs, have been helped through the ministry of the mission and many were brought to Christ.

This beautiful hymn penned by Horatio Spafford has provided comfort and inspiration to others. God has used their sorrow to glorify His name and advance the Kingdom in a major way. Just before he wrote that great hymn, Spafford wrote these words in a letter.

"On Thursday we passed over the spot where she went down, in mid-ocean, the water three miles deep. But I do not think of our dear ones there. They are safe, folded, the dear lambs, and there, before very long, shall we be too. In the meantime, thanks to God, we have an opportunity to serve and praise Him for His love and mercy to us and ours. I will praise Him while I have my being. May we each one arise, leave all, and follow Him."

A modern-day Hero of Faith story.

As I read a book entitled *Grace Enough for Three*, my heart breaks in many different ways. This poignant book penned by a friend of our family, Don Clifford, tells us about the all-sufficient grace of God. As you read this summary, I think you will see how the Cliffords would fit into the Hall of Fame of Faith Heroes.

After giving birth to a sweet baby girl in 1961, named Vicki, almost exactly a year later, their son Mike was born. At 2 ½ years old, they lost their son. They found him lifeless in his bed. You can only imagine this trauma if it has happened to you. It was only because of their faith and God's grace they were able to rebuild their life.

With the decision to increase their family, Karen became pregnant right away, but miscarried in the ninth week. Within months, Karen was pregnant again, only to miscarry at 4 ½ months.

(Can you even imagine the discouragement, pain, and emotional draining they must have experienced in losing a 2 ½ year old son and then two miscarriages right away?)

They both continued in their walk and their faith grew as they served in their church and studied and taught the Bible.

In 1968 their daughter Rebecca was born. Two years after Becky was born, another daughter, Rachel arrived on the scene. The Cliffords were basking in joy that was coming from the love of children.

Five years after their son Mike died, the path of their spiritual pilgrimage turned back into that familiar but unwelcomed valley of the shadow of death. Rachel had contracted meningitis and developed brain damage. For the next couple of years she would have convulsions, be in and out of hospitals with frequent resuscitations. In 1974, at 3 ½ years old, God released Rachel from her damaged body. How could this be? How much more can we take? Does God even care? How do we get through this storm? An array of many more questions flooded the minds of Don and Karen Clifford.

It was John 14:27-28 that Don and Karen used to comfort their broken hearts. Don writes in his book how he closed his eyes and let the Holy Spirit minister to his soul.

> *"Let not your hearts be troubled. You believe in God, believe also in me."*
>
> *"Peace I leave with you; my peace I give to you...Do not let your hearts be troubled and do not be afraid...if you loved me, you would be glad that I am going to the Father."*

Don said he felt the Lord saying to him, "If you love Rachel, you should be glad she has gone to the Father."

The Cliffords, being Heroes of Faith, gave thanks for the three years they had with Rachel as they will always remember them as some of the happiest days of their lives.

A year after Rachel's death, Beth was born into this family. One day while feeding Beth a bottle, her facial features distorted slightly and she froze with a blank stare. This was a familiar sight. These same seizures took their son's life. These seizures did not affect Beth's growth physically or mentally. She was a normal, happy busy child, but they just couldn't control the seizures. When Beth was five years old, they left her with her older sister Becky just for an hour. In her care, with no warning, Beth had a massive seizure. It was only days later, Don and Karen again, said goodbye to a precious child. They entered to what they deemed as fighting their most difficult battle of faith.

I don't even know how to end this story. To have seven pregnancies, five children, and three die before the age of six, is more than I thought anyone could handle. However, because of their faith in a good God, and His sufficient grace, they continue to praise God and serve Him. The Clifford's have coauthored a companion book entitled *Heavenly Grief, a Christian Guide to Spiritual and Emotional Healing.*

I know many of you have a story that would qualify you to be introduced as a "Hero of Faith." I hope these stories and lessons will encourage you to ask God to help you with your unbelief and become a Broken Warrior with great faith!

Preparing For Battle
ক্ষেত্ৰ

Read Mark 9:14-29, Matthew 17:14-21 and Luke 9:37-43. This is the same story but three different Authors.

What is common in all three stories?

_____

_____

_____

What were the disciples lacking?

_____

_____

_____

Why do you think the story is not written with the same detail in Matthew and Luke as it is in Mark?

_____

_____

_____

How do you deal with doubts about your faith?

_____

_____

_____

What piece of armor would you wear to help you with doubts about God?

_____

_____

_____

What specifically will you do to start becoming a Broken Warrior with great faith?

_____

_____

_____

Weapons of Truth

Memorize:

"Have faith in God," Jesus answered. "I tell you the truth, if anyone says to this mountain, 'Go, throw yourself into the sea,' and does not doubt in his heart but believes that what he says will happen, it will be done for him. Therefore I tell you, whatever you ask for in prayer, believe that you have received it, and it will be yours" (Mark 11:22-24).

Digging Deeper

Read Mark 9:14-16

Where were Jesus, Peter, James and John coming from?

_____

_____

_____

Why do you think the disciples were arguing?

_____

_____

_____

Mark 9:19-21

Whom is Jesus talking to?

_____

_____

_____

What do you think he meant when He said "How long shall I put up with you?"

_____

_____

_____

Why did Jesus ask the boy's father "How long has he been like this?"

_____

_____

_____

Mark 9:29

What was the reason the disciples couldn't drive out the demon?

_____

_____

_____

What spoke most to you from this passage?

_____

_____

_____

Further Reading

Psalms 6:9
Psalm 17:1
1 Corinthians 7:5
1 Peter 3:12
Psalm 5:1-3
Luke 6:12
James 5:16-18

Chapter 5
ಶಿ ಶಿ ಶಿ

Clothed in Humility

"All of you clothe yourselves with humility toward one another, because, 'God opposes the proud but gives grace to the humble.'"

(1 Peter 5:5b)

Deep Thoughts

*A flea is riding on an elephant, after crossing an old bridge, says, "Did you notice how we shook that bridge?"

*Peter Marshall once said, "Lord, when we are wrong, make us willing to change. When we are right, make us easy to live with."

*Humility is like underwear; we should have it but not let it show.

* We have plenty of people nowadays who could not kill a mouse without publishing it in the gospel gazette. Samson killed a lion and said nothing about it: the Holy Spirit finds modesty so rare that He takes care to record it. Say much of

what the Lord has done for you, but say little of what you have done for the Lord. Do not utter a self-glorifying sentence. *Charles Spurgeon*

*Water always fills the lowest places first. So the lower, the emptier a man lies before God, the speedier and the fuller the inflow of the divine glory will be.

*Humility is not thinking less of yourself, but thinking of yourself less.

*Humility is the highest lesson a believer has to learn.

*When we come to the end of ourselves we come to the beginning of God. *Billy Graham*

*Humility is not denying the power you have. It is realizing that the power comes through you, not from you.
Fred Smith

*The branch that bears the most fruit is bent the lowest to the ground.

One of my favorite stories of pride avoidance comes from Mother Teresa. A reporter came to her after she had won the Nobel Peace Prize. He asked her if she was worried that all the public acclaim she was receiving would go to her head and she would become proud. She paused and said, "Do you remember the time Jesus rode into Jerusalem on the back of a donkey and all the people were shouting 'Hosanna!' and waving palm branches and throwing their clothes down to make a path?" The reporter said, "Yes, I do."

Mother Teresa then said in her quiet way, "Do you think the donkey thought it was for him?"

We are but donkeys who carry the Christ. All eyes should be on him, and not us.

One Sunday morning, years ago, I had the privilege to get to teach the three year olds. It was a beautiful fall morning and the kids were full of energy as they came into the classroom. I was not their regular teacher so I was anxious to make them feel comfortable and make some new friends. Now I love kids, just not sure my niche is teaching preschoolers. However, I was up for the challenge. Jacob came strolling in with perfectly cut blond hair, red plaid shirt, tan corduroy pants and his brown boots. He had big blue eyes that greeted me with a smile. I said, "Good morning Jacob, you sure look great today." We were off to a good start.

It wasn't long and we all settled together in a circle in those itty bitty chairs. I started teaching the lesson for the day. As I told the story of how Jesus can make us feel better, how He is the healer of all our hurts, I was careful to use the right language a child would understand. I used terms like, boo-boos, instead of wounds. That is what brilliant teachers do. After I told the story, the kids walked away mesmerized and so full of knowledge...I was sure. Except for Jacob, I could tell he didn't understand anything I had just so carefully said. I bent down and proceeded to explain the story again except this time I used a prop to help illustrate my point. I said "Jacob, hold out your hand." He held his little hand out in front of me, I proceeded to put a band-aid on his hand and said "You see Jacob, Jesus can heal our hurts, our boo-boos. He covers them like this band-aid." Do you understand? He glanced at me and smiled, shook his head as though he did and then went to the other side of the room to play with some toys. I had done it! I had met the challenge of teaching children about God. I am a great teacher!

Until...his mother came to pick him up. She walked in the classroom and began to ask me how things went with Jacob. I said, "He is so adorable and smart, we had a great time." Just then Jacob saw his mom from across the room and started running towards her, with his arm outstretched screaming, "Mommy, Mommy." She bent down and said, "What's wrong Jacob?" Jacob held his arm up to show her the band-aid on his hand, and just when I thought he was going to tell her the story and what a brilliant teacher I was, he then proclaimed, "Look, Jesus bit me!"

Hmmm, maybe I'm not the teacher I thought I was. I haven't been asked back to teach the three year olds since.

Unforgettable Humility

"Now that I, your Lord and Teacher, have washed your feet, you also should wash one another's feet" (John 13:14).

Besides the cross, the most humbling act in the Bible is Jesus' washing the disciples' feet. This act of humility has so much depth we could talk about this verse for months.

This great lesson was performed just before the Passover Feast at the "Last Supper." Jesus got up from the supper table, from the meal, and prepared to wash the disciples' feet. This menial task was usually performed by a Gentile slave. However, this time Jesus washed and dried each of their feet. I just can't imagine the disciples didn't weep and their hearts had to be bursting with joy. (I have attended an event where this humbling act is re-enacted and it is powerful. Visit www.deepbreathministries.com).

We need this lesson of humility. This profound act teaches us love and true humility grows out of our relationship with the Father. If our desire is to glorify God, and be in His will, then let's follow His example and serve others.

Warrior Weapon

Humbly serve others!

Dear Diary

Do you keep a diary? Maybe you call it a journal. I started writing in a journal only about five years ago. I had tried several times before. I bought a beautiful tapestry-covered journal and the perfect pen to inspire me, but when I opened the book, the blank page just stared at me as if to say, "I dare you." One of my first Bible study teachers, Betty, gave me a journal as a gift for helping with the administration duties of the class, and she wrote a special "Thank You" in the cover of the journal. This encouragement inspired me to start writing down my prayers and thoughts about God. Never once did I think I would be writing down how God spoke to me. I learned there is no right way or wrong way to write in your personal journal. There *is* healing, however, and my prayers stayed focused by writing them down. In addition, to be able to go back and read my "road traveled" has been priceless.

I also noticed a definite pattern in my prayers. They seem to be asking the same thing for every situation. Many lines began with "Help Me." This introduction of every sentence many times was followed by the word "pride." I hope some of my following journal entries bring insight to you.

Journal Entry, February 16

"To keep me from becoming conceited because of these
surpassingly great revelations, there was given me a thorn

in my flesh, a messenger of Satan, to torment me. Three times I pleaded with the Lord to take it away from me. But he said to me, 'My grace is sufficient for you, for my power is made perfect in weakness.' Therefore I will boast all the more gladly about my weaknesses, so that Christ's power may rest on me. That is why, for Christ's sake, I delight in weaknesses, in insults, in hardships, in persecutions, in difficulties. For when I am weak, then I am strong" (2 Corinthians 12:7-10).

"Do nothing out of selfish ambition or vain conceit, but in humility consider others better than yourselves" (Philippians 2:3).

Lord, please don't let my thorn be debilitating, but enough to remind me. It is all about you, it's not about me. It's not about my pride, but all about your truth.

Journal Entry, April 14

"'The terror you inspire and the pride of your heart have deceived you, you who live in the clefts of the rocks, who occupy the heights of the hill. Though you build your nest as high as the eagle's, from there I will bring you down,' declares the LORD" (Jeremiah 49:16).

Father, your gifts you give me, the ambition, drive and passion, may it all be used for Kingdom purposes and not for me or the world. Thank you for Your Word.

Journal Entry, May 17

Lord, I cry to you. I praise you. My heart hurts.

What is the difference between "Please help me" and "I need you Jesus"? In one word, *Humility.*

Help me with my doubts

I need you Jesus

Help me with my insecurities

I need you Jesus

Help me with thoughts that only glorify you

I need you Jesus

Help me with my fears

I need you Jesus

Help me to want tomorrow

I need you Jesus

Help me with today

I need you Jesus

Help me with my enemies

I need you Jesus

Help me with my faith

I need you Jesus

Help me to seek you with all my heart, soul and mind

  I need you Jesus

Help me to live everyday in your presence

  I need you Jesus

Help me to accept your great love

  I need you Jesus

Thank you Father for your promise.

"Cast your cares on the Lord and he will sustain you; He will never let the righteous fall" (Psalm 55:22).

Journal Entry, February 12

Lord, am I constantly humiliating You? I don't want to ignore you Lord. I don't deliberately mean to disobey you. It must be fear of conviction. After reading Exodus 20:19,

> *"and said to Moses, 'Speak to us yourself and we will listen. But do not have God speak to us or we will die.'"*

I see it is easier to listen to one of your servants instead of you directly. This way my obedience seems optional. Lord, I want to obey and listen to You! Thank you for your grace.

Journal Entry, November 1

This poem written by Beth Moore depicts pride perfectly.

  My name is Pride. I am a cheater.

I cheat you of your God-given destiny...because you demand your own way.

I cheat you of contentment...because you "deserve better than this."

I cheat you of knowledge...because you already know it all.

I cheat you of healing...because you're too full of me to forgive.

I cheat you of holiness...because you refuse to admit when you're wrong.

I cheat you of vision...because you'd rather look in the mirror than out a window.

I cheat you of genuine friendship...because nobody's going to know the real you.

I cheat you of love...because real romance demands sacrifice.

I cheat you of greatness in heaven...because you refuse to wash another's feet on earth.

I cheat you of God's glory...because I convince you to seek your own.

My name is Pride. I am a cheater.

You like me because you think I'm always looking out for you. Untrue.

I'm looking to make a fool of you.

God has so much for you, _____ (put your name here) I admit, but don't worry...

If you stick with me

You'll never know.

Father, thank you for Your words of truth. I need you! I need you Holy Spirit, keep me from the "cheater."

Warrior Weapon

Start a Journal to record praise and prayers, and God's Word to me.

> *"The relationship between God and believer must be marked by humility. Humility is the only soil in which the graces take root; the lack of humility is the sufficient explanation of every defect and failure."*   Andrew Murray, *Humility*

Pride-ful to Pride-less

"Take my yoke upon you and learn from me, for I am gentle and humble in heart, and you will find rest for your souls" (Matthew 11:29).

"Not so with you. Instead, whoever wants to become great among you must be your servant and whoever wants to be first must be your slave just as the Son of Man did not come

to be served, but to serve, and to give his life as a ransom for many" (Matthew 20:26-28).

"I live in a high and holy place, but also with him who is contrite and lowly in spirit, to revive the spirit of the lowly and to revive the heart of the contrite" (Isaiah 57:15).

"A man's pride brings him low, but a man of lowly spirit gains honor" (Proverbs 29:23.)

We might humble ourselves before God, but are we showing humility to our fellow man? Humility is what we carry not only in prayer but in our words and actions of everyday life.

Here are some suggestions of moving from pride-full to pride-less:

*Understanding the Cross

> The sacrifice of Christ alone should be enough. Everything I have, everything I am, every good thing I enjoy would not be possible were it not for Him. The more we understand the price He paid, the less room we have for pride. (Romans 6:6)

*Give Thanks

> A heart filled with gratitude cannot be anything but humble (another great reason for the Praise Journal). (Psalm 136:1)

*Attitude

>As Broken Warriors, our attitude should be of one that enables us to lay aside our rights in order to serve others. (Philippians 2:5)

*Serving

>The most powerful decision we can make in our life is to do something for someone who doesn't have the power or resources to return the favor. (Galatians 5:13)

Benefits of serving: (adapted from *A Purpose Driven Life* by Rick Warren)

>*Servants will think more about others than themselves.
>
>*Servants will begin to think more like stewards rather than owners.
>
>*Servants will think about their work instead of comparing, criticizing or competing with others.
>
>*Servants will begin to base their identity in Christ.

Maybe the attitude should be not waiting to "heal to serve" but to "serve to heal."

Serving = Humility

> *Our goal is to make God look good, not ourselves.*

The warning of pride is weaved throughout all of scripture, but so are the rewards of humility. The benefits of being humble include:

> *You are Considered by God (Psalm 138:6)
>
> *You are Heard by God (Psalm 9:12)
>
> *You are Delivered by God (Job 22:29)
>
> *You are Lifted up by God (James 4:10)
>
> *You are Exalted by God (Luke 14:11)
>
> *You are to Receive more Grace (James 4:6)

Warrior Weapon

Become occupied with God!

Unguarded Moments

It is in our unguarded moments when our real character reveals itself. An unguarded moment is like Galatians 5:17 describes, "*For the sinful nature desires what is contrary to the Spirit, and the Spirit what is contrary to the sinful nature. They are in conflict with each other, so that you do not do what you want."* These moments always have pride attached to them. What does "unguarded moments" mean to you? Can you think of something you did or said recently which had pride written all over it? Or maybe you have been the victim of an "unguarded moment." These "unguarded moments" can and have literally ruined lives.

Peter, the eager, bold, impulsive, confident disciple, who was with Jesus and saw miracles performed, professed Jesus was the Christ, had several "unguarded moments." One in particular, in Luke 22:22-24. The disciples and Jesus are sitting down, well actually they are reclining, at dinner (the Last Supper) and to paraphrase, Jesus says, one of you that is sitting with me will betray me. Verse 23 explains what the disciples did next:

> *"They began to question among themselves which of them it might be who would do this. Also a dispute arose among them as to which of them was considered to be greatest."*

Now this was not an ordinary, everyday dinner; this was right before the most important event in human history took place. Those prideful disciples showed no expression of concern at all for Jesus. The disciples actually began to argue about who was the greatest among them, jockeying for power and position. There they sat in the physical presence of Jesus, yet their eyes were on themselves. Theologians have said most likely Simon Peter started the argument because he was the most outspoken and confident. His name was always listed first in Matthew, Mark, Luke and Acts, an indication of him being the leader of the Twelve. However, his confidence in this story is not rooted in love but pride.

I am sure Peter said something to trigger someone else's ego, then he shot his mouth off, and away they went. Have you ever had that happen? You think you are anchored in love, and then someone who hasn't had this study yet and is full of pride says something that pierces your ego, maybe not even intentionally, just because they are so full of pride. They are not thinking of hurting you, just how they can lift themselves up. However, they pierced your ego and you retaliate. And so on, and so on.

I wondered if Judas was part of that argument at the dinner table. What do you think Judas was thinking, especially since Jesus had just committed the humbling act of washing his feet? Was Peter any different from Judas? As the story goes, Judas betrays Jesus, Jesus is arrested, and eventually led to crucifixion. After His arrest, Peter is asked three times if he knows Jesus, and Peter denies knowing Him each time.

Here's the difference between Peter and Judas. When Jesus was crucified, Judas had feelings of despair, even remorse, not because of what he did to Jesus, but because of what it did to him. Unfortunately, Judas had not grabbed hold of the truth, he was still an unbeliever. Judas is a great reminder for us, it is possible to be near Christ yet still not know Him. Since Judas was an unbeliever, he did not have the Shield of Faith to ward off Satan's attacks. As it clearly says in John 13:27, *"As soon as Judas took the bread, Satan entered into him."* Judas knew he had sinned, but his pride (Satan) kept him from knowing the goodness and grace of Christ. Judas's inward glare at himself had reached an all-time low. Although he did have a change of heart after Jesus was condemned, Judas was seized with remorse, returned the thirty silver coins, then hanged himself. His pride kept him from knowing God's grace and now it would keep him from life.

Peter loved the Lord. He was remorseful, ashamed and had feelings of great despair that he had denied knowing Jesus three times. However, Peter knew of God's grace, he had experienced it. Peter might have been downhearted and ready to give up but allowed himself to be transformed. He *let* Jesus change him.

Peter acted like most Christians do today. Sometimes spiritual; sometimes not so much. Sometimes following the flesh; sometimes functioning in the Spirit. Peter was rooted and grounded in God's love, which is deep and wide, long and high. And so it is the same for us.

> *"I pray that out of His glorious riches He may strengthen you with power through His Spirit in your inner being, so that Christ may dwell in your hearts through faith. And I pray that you, being rooted and established in love, may*

have power, together with all the saints, to grasp how wide and long and high and deep is the love of Christ" (Ephesians 3:16-18).

To summarize our unguarded moments, I have bad news and good news. The bad news is, we will never completely get over ourselves. We will always have the thorn of pride in our side, until Heaven. The good news is, our God saves. He transforms. He has sufficient grace. Our road to humility is not taken alone.

"And hope does not disappoint us, because God has poured out his love into our hearts by the Holy Spirit, whom he has given us" (Romans 5:5).

"Humble yourselves, therefore, under God's mighty hand, that he may lift you up in due time" (1 Peter 5:6).

Warrior Weapon

"Let not the foot of pride come upon me" (Psalm 36:11).

Pride is the only disease known to man that makes everyone sick except the one who has it.

Come To Me

I tend to be a big-picture thinker, which leads to grandiose ideas. This is not a bad thing for the right situation; however, to be grandiose in everything takes its toll. Because of pride, I used to think when God and I talked, He was going to tell me to do something BIG. In reading Matthew 11:28 where Jesus says, *"Come to me, all you who are weary and burdened, and I will give you rest,"* I noticed the comma after "Come to me." Comma means pause. What He means is just that, Come to Me! Not "come to me" just *if* you are weary and burdened, or only *when* you are sick. Or only in our deepest need and darkest hour, *but always, for everything, all the time.*

I will admit, this invitation steps on my pride. This would mean I have to be humbled enough to go to Him for EVERYTHING. However, that is exactly what He is commanding. What is keeping you from going to Him? Do we not trust Him enough? Is it a matter of showing our weakness if we go to Him for ALL our needs? Whatever stronghold it is, it's the very thing God can release you from if you will do as He commands: *"Come to Me."*

The journey from pride to humility can be a long and treacherous road. Just so you know, no matter where you started, the journey never ends, at least not here on earth. However, when occupied with God and filled with His love, it is a journey you don't want to miss.

My friends, let's leave this chapter committing ourselves to be humble servants, to guard our thoughts and words. For our soul to be so filled with His presence, there is no room for self. The result will be, He will be exalted!

> *"Human pride will be humbled,*
> *and human arrogance will be brought down.*
> *Only the LORD will be exalted*
> *on that day of judgment"* (Isaiah 2:17 NLT).

Warrior Weapon

Go to Him for EVERYTHING!

Prayer for Humility

Father God, I praise you! Thank you Lord for you are my Deliverer, my strength in whom I trust. You have the power to set me free and transform my life. Lord I pray that you make me simple, draw me to you. Take from my heart every kind and form of pride. Awaken in me the deepest depth of humility. Help me to clothe myself with humility toward others. I desire to humble myself before You and trust that You will lift me up. You are Holy Lord, and praise will remain on my lips. I love you Father, Amen.

Preparing for Battle
ôôô

Read and record the following verses:

> *You are Considered by God (Psalm 138:6)
> *You are Heard by God (Psalm 9:12)
> *You are Delivered by God (Job 22:29)
> *You are Lifted up by God (James 4:10)
> *You are Exalted by God (Luke 14:11)
> *You are to Receive more Grace (James 4:6)

When was your last "unguarded moment"? What will you do to prepare against these "unguarded moments"?

_____

_____

_____

How will you stay occupied with God?

_____

_____

_____

What is keeping you from going to God for everything?

_____

_____

_____

What is the greatest lesson you learned from this chapter?

_____

_____

_____

Weapons of Truth

Memorize:

"All of you, clothe yourselves with humility toward one another, because, 'God opposes the proud but gives grace to the humble.' Humble yourselves, therefore, under God's mighty hand, that He may lift you up in due time"
(1 Peter 5:5-6).

I have an obsession with crosses. I have many hanging in my bedroom, living room, and office walls. They are beautiful. They are all unique and I do admire them. I am looking at these crosses with a different perspective. They will be a reminder to me of the sacrifice and the humiliation Jesus suffered. I will use these crosses to remind me to:

*Purposefully seek humility.
*All we have been given comes from God.
*He loves me, Just as I am.

What object can be a reminder to you to have daily humility?

_____

_____

_____

What three points will you take from this chapter?

_____

_____

_____

Digging Deeper

Read about "The Last Supper" in all four Gospels.

Note the differences from each account.

_____

_____

_____

Was Judas at the table when the argument of who was the greatest broke out?

_____

_____

_____

Read Luke 14:7-11 and Luke 18:9-14.

What do these two passages teach us about humility?

_____

_____

_____

Chapter 6
❧❧❧

Strength Will Rise as We Wait upon the Lord

"But those who wait on the LORD
Shall renew their strength;
They shall mount up with wings like eagles,
They shall run and not be weary,
They shall walk and not faint" (Isaiah 40:31, NKJV).

"KNOCK, KNOCK." "Who's there?" "IMPATIENT CHICKEN." "Impatien*" "CLUCK."*

That is how much patience I have. Yes it is true. If I am behind you at a traffic light, it turns green and you don't move instantly, don't be surprised when you hear a quick "honk"(not a lay-on-the-horn honk for I do that only if I have to). I even have to get psyched up every couple of weeks to sit and wait while I get my nails done. Although what should be a luxury is irritating to me because of how long it takes, but not as much as having messy nails. I mean I am the one who stands in front of a microwave, while it is cooking a full-course meal in three minutes, shouting, "C'mon, hurry up!"

As I have gotten older, I have become more patient. In my defense, however, I want to blame the world some for magnifying this issue. We live in what I call "a microwave world." We don't wait for anything. Is the term 'waiting patiently" even used these days? We can now have movies on demand in our living room; we don't have to wait until they come out on DVD. We eat many of our meals from a bag and in our car. We have self-checkout at grocery stores so we don't have to wait in line. I also remember when my Dad would change the oil in the car and it would take about an hour. Now if you can spare 10 minutes, you get your oil changed, windows washed, and air in your tires. There is even on-line speed dating. Because of technology, much has changed in the last twenty years.

What hasn't changed is being in God's "waiting room." As Believers of Christ, God is always concerned about us and wants to bless us. Sometimes this requires us waiting for Him and His direction.

The Waiting Room

"Be still before the LORD and wait patiently for Him" (Psalm 37:7).

>   *All the spiritual disciplines have their value, but it is in God's *waiting* room where patience and dependence are taught.

*Nowhere is there a better place for cultivating patience than in *waiting* on God. It is in His waiting room where we discover how impatient we are and what our impatience means.

*Waiting is to teach us our absolute dependence upon God's mighty works.

*By *resting* in Him and *waiting* for Him, this honors God greatly. It yields [our] self wholly into His hands. It lets God be God.

*It has been said, "Your failure has been due to only one thing. You sought to conquer and obey in your own strength."

*Waiting on God will become the renewal of your strength.

*The privilege of *waiting* upon God, brings great responsibility.

Warrior Weapon

Wait patiently for the Lord.

Strength Will Rise

Several years ago, I claimed Isaiah 40:31 as my life verse. At the time, this verse really spoke to me and has become the foundation and namesake of the ministry God has called me to, *Choose To Soar Ministries.* What is interesting to me is as I grow in my relationship with the Lord, He continues to reveal Himself more and more through this verse. The lesson is: don't think you can read a verse a couple of times and get all the meaning it holds. Scripture is the gift that keeps on giving. Scripture has only one truth, but many applications. Let's explore how this verse applies to the concept of waiting.

"But those who wait on the LORD
Shall renew their strength;
They shall mount up with wings like eagles,
They shall run and not be weary,
They shall walk and not faint" (Isaiah 40:31, NKJV).

The prophet Isaiah is a great example of someone waiting on the promises of God. The book of Isaiah, is also known as the "Fifth Gospel" because of its prophecies that were filled in the New Testament. Now that is definitely a whole other study, but it is fun to see the predictions of the coming Messiah in the book of Isaiah, about 700 years before Jesus, and then watch them unfold.

A short synopsis of Isaiah is; Isaiah's role was to be a deliverer of God's messages to his fellow Jews. He told them and warned them about God's punishment if they did not repent and turn to God. In fact, the first 39 chapters are all about the warning of what is to come and they had better straighten up, or else! The rest of Isaiah speaks of God's comfort and the upcoming Messiah who will save them all and restore the nation. (I find it interesting that there are 66 chapters in Isaiah, as there are 66 books in the Bible).

Let's zoom in to verses 40:27-30 (NLT):

> *27 O Jacob, how can you say the LORD does not see your troubles? O Israel, how can you say God ignores your rights? 28 Have you never heard? Have you never understood? The LORD is the everlasting God, the Creator of all the earth. He never grows weak or weary. No one can measure the depths of his understanding. 29 He gives power to the weak and strength to the powerless. 30 Even youths will become weak and tired, and young men will fall in exhaustion.*

The Jews are complaining to God and questioning if He knows what is really going on. They continue to whine about how He doesn't care about them. What a bunch of babies. The Jews, being consumed with their own circumstances, never stopped to listen and missed what Isaiah was telling them. Isaiah is trying to explain to them about the Lord's empowering strength; if only, they would wait, trust, and hope in the Lord. (In the different translations, wait, hope, and trust are all interchangeable in verse 31).

Isaiah had to be frustrated and discouraged with his fellow Jews but I am thinking maybe also with God? I wonder if Isaiah knew he was in God's waiting room.

Can we pause here a second and ask ourselves if maybe we might look like those Jews? Do we think that sometimes God must not be paying attention to our situation? Does He really care? On the other hand, maybe when God asks us to do what we think is impossible (give up control of our kids, spouse, a situation), we don't have the strength to let go? Think about that. Do you have the *strength to let go?*

> *"Each time he said, 'My grace is all you need. My power works best in weakness.' So now I am glad to boast about my weaknesses, so that the power of Christ can work through me.* **10***That's why I take pleasure in my weaknesses, and in the insults, hardships, persecutions, and troubles that I suffer for Christ. For when I am weak, then I am strong"* (2 Corinthians 12:9-10 NLT).

As Broken Warriors, we must choose to accept God's grace and strength. We can do this! God's promises of His strength are woven throughout the Bible.

"I can do everything through Him who gives me strength" (Philippians 4:13).

My friend Karyn Brownlee writes a great blog (www.brighterwalk.com). Once she wrote about how her daughter had a bumper sticker on the back of her car that read, "Live Weak." Karyn was confused; we all know the slogan is "Live Strong." But it was her daughter who got it right. As Christians, we must remember in whose strength we are to live.

When we trust ourselves, when we get impatient, we will get weary, we will fall. But...

> *"those who wait on the LORD*
> *Shall renew their strength;*
> *They shall mount up with wings like eagles,*
> *They shall run and not be weary,*
> *They shall walk and not faint"* (Isaiah 40:31, NKJV).

The wait does not mean we sit and eat Oreos and do nothing. Believe me, I've tried.

As I mentioned before, the word "wait" is interchangeable in other translations for "hope" and "trust." To "wait," to "hope" or "trust" in the Lord, is looking to Him for all our needs. Which also means His ways and His timing are perfect.

When He tells us He will renew our strength when we wait, God means He will "exchange" our weakness for His power. Like the eagle, this is how we are able to soar above the storms. With His strength, you will be able to run through the challenges and walk with faith in the daily demands.

What do you need to release from your hands? What is keeping you from the "exchange of His power for your weakness?" What is keeping you from soaring?

"The greatest heroes of faith are not always those who seem to be soaring; often it is they who are patiently plodding. As we wait on the Lord, He enables us not only to fly higher and run faster, but also to walk longer. Blessed are the plodders, for they eventually arrive at their destination."
Warren Wiersbe

In waiting on him, we will find rest and joy and strength and the supply of every need.

A few years ago, I used a personal trainer to get healthy. The great thing about a trainer is they push you when you think you can't possibly do any more. When you are doing weight training, the muscle has to be pushed to exhaustion for it to be strengthened. It is always the last two or three repetitions that cause this exhaustion. When I worked out by myself, I would always quit before I needed to do those last two or three reps. This is exactly what my spiritually deep friend Brenda Cox meant when she told me, "Tanya, it is one thing to put yourself on the cross and another when He puts you on the cross." [From Chapter 1] We get impatient and "take ourselves down" before we can be strengthened. We get tired, weak and want to be in control.

The next time you are in God's waiting room, what will you do to make sure you wait, trust, hope in God's strength?

Warrior Weapon

"Live Weak!"

Your Attention Please!

What do you picture in your mind when you feel like you are waiting on God? Do you picture yourself sitting in a chair and waiting? Are you in your car, or at church? What are you doing while you are waiting to hear from Him? Could it be that God is the one sitting and waiting for you? Are you even aware that He is trying to get your attention? Could it be the busyness of your life has left no opportunity for paying attention to how He is talking to you? Then we wonder why we haven't heard from Him.

I believe sometimes we are not in the "waiting room," we just think we are because we have missed all the ways God is trying to communicate with us. Metaphorically, we are **outside** the waiting room, pacing the halls, wondering where He is.

The story is of a woman who was caught in a great flood. The waters were rising quickly. Some neighbors came by to help her but she refused to leave and said she was waiting on God to rescue her. As the intensity of the situation arose, so did the water and she found herself clinging to the shingles on top of her roof. A police rescue team came by at this time in a small boat to help her. She again refused and proclaimed she was waiting on God's provision. It wasn't long when a Coast Guard helicopter came overhead and let a ladder down for her as the last resort to grab and cling to, but you guessed it, she refused and had faith God would save her. Well, the waters washed her away and there she stood at the Gates of Heaven with a surprised look on her face. As she meets the Lord, she says, "Lord, I waited for you, why didn't you rescue me?" The Lord responded, "I ran out of patience."

We know that God doesn't run out of patience; I am living proof of that. However, don't you think we are guilty of responding like the woman on the roof? She was waiting unnecessarily. It is one thing to wait on God, it is another to not be paying attention. We only think we are waiting on God because His provision looks different than ours.

God desires to communicate with us and wants us to listen. We know He has a willingness to communicate with us because of the various methods He has used. For example: He used dreams to speak with Joseph, Isaiah, and Jacob; angels to speak to Mary, Zechariah, and Shepherds. He wrote on the wall to get Belshazzar's attention and burned a bush for Moses. He had Jonah spend some time in the belly of a whale. He made a donkey talk to Balaam. God spoke audibly to Abraham, Moses, Paul, and Jesus. Most notably, God used His Son to speak to us. How is God speaking to you? Do you think God isn't trying? I believe He is, we just are not paying attention, we are not watching for Him. We are busy, weary, drained from life's trials and just don't spend enough time learning to hear God's voice in the midst of it all.

God will always meet us where we are, we just need to pay attention. I love the classic story of two of His followers who are walking down the road to the village Emmaus (Luke 24:13-35). This story takes place the afternoon of the discovery of the empty tomb. Some followers of His were discouraged, full of disappointment and focused on their problems. They were so consumed with their own issues, Jesus appears and walks along side them, and they don't recognize him. Jesus enters into a conversation with them, He asks what they are discussing. Cleopas says, "What are you nuts, haven't you heard about the things that have happened the last three days?" What I think is funny is the humorous way Jesus responded, "What things?" You can see the smile on Jesus' face when He said those words. These followers knew Jesus had risen, but were not paying attention or watching for Him. Even after Jesus responded, they still didn't know it was Him. Oh my goodness! Their consuming thoughts of themselves almost makes them miss the solution for their problems. It isn't until meal time when their eyes were opened and they recognized Him. Then, He disappeared. It took an ordinary activity to slow their minds and take time to notice their inner stirring which in verse 32: "*Were not our hearts burning within us while he was talking to us on the road?*"

Are you paying attention on *your road* to Emmaus? "*The practice of paying attention awakens us to what is extraordinary in the midst of the ordinary.*" Ruth Haley Barton

Warrior Weapon

Look for the Lord in every situation.

Perfect Timing

There are two types of waiting. One is the "I can hardly wait," waiting. This includes things like:

> Opening presents on your birthday or Christmas
>
> Your wedding day
>
> Your child or grandchild to be born
>
> Graduation
>
> Thanksgiving Dinner

The other type is, the "I'm so tired of waiting." This waiting can make you cry, scared, and weary. These include waiting for things like:

> The lab results
>
> A hardened heart to change in a relationship
>
> For employment
>
> To be adopted
>
> The light for your dark world
>
> To be loved by someone

Some of us are waiting to die and some of us are waiting to live. I am not sure which is worse.

I know some of you have been waiting a long time to see some change. Spending time in God's "waiting room" has got to be the hardest thing we are called to do. However, God does keep His promises; we have to learn to wait and rest in His perfect timing.

Speaking of perfect timing, on my previous trip to the "waiting room," I would read in the Bible about others who waited on God's renewal, and His promises. I can't say that was the best idea at the time. What I mean is, to be honest, I didn't get encouraged by reading where Abraham waited 24 years for his promise to become a father. And I don't even want to talk about the 40 years Moses waited in the desert.

But as I continued to read the Bible for encouragement and understanding, I was reminded about Noah. The story we know of

Noah is common. He built an ark out of obedience to God's direction. God flooded the earth by sending rain for 40 days and nights. Noah and his family and array of animals, floated in these waters. This story is in Genesis, but let me direct you to a particular verse which really caught my eye.

> *"The animals going in were male and female of every living thing, as God had commanded Noah. THEN THE LORD SHUT HIM IN"* (Genesis 7:16 NIV).

Oh my! Did you get that, the Lord closed the door behind him. Now what did the author of Genesis mean by that statement? I am relatively sure God wasn't physically there. So how is this verse encouraging? It's encouraging to me because this told me God will put us in places for awhile because it is best for us and in His plan. It also tells me God will protect us while we are in our "ark." Our task, our responsibility, our purpose, is to wait.

Imagine being Noah, you are in a boat with your spouse, kids and hundreds of animals. First couple of days might have seemed like quite an adventure and I am sure Noah was patting himself on the back because he obeyed God by building the Ark and as a result he and his family were saved from the tragic flood.

However, I am thinking Noah's journal probably read something like this;

Day 5---the rain is really coming down but the boat is handling the waters great. I have to say I did a great job in building this beauty.

Day 10---the rain hasn't let up any. But that's okay; our family time together is great.

Day 20---still raining. Getting tired of eating the same ole stuff, the two pigs are starting to look really good. I hope this rain stops soon; the family is starting to get on my nerves.

Day 25---still raining! This boat really isn't as big as I first thought. I wish I had brought the *Febreze.*

Day 30---**still raining!!** God was serious about this "flooding the earth" thing. I have looked out the one and only window and trust me, there is no land in sight; it is all gone, nothing but water. Did He really say *40* days and nights?

Day 35--- you guessed it, still raining! Okay, now that is enough! How unfair is this!!! I did exactly what God told me to do. We sacrificed a lot as a family in obedience to God. The Mrs. was shunned from the "garden club," Noah Jr. was tormented at school by the other kids because his father was building a large boat on dry land, and the guys thought I had carried this fellowship thing with God too far. And THIS is the thanks I get??

Day 39----this stinkin' rain has led me to no other choice but to hit the bottle. If I have to have another talk with the boys about chasing the elephants again, somebody is gonna get hurt.

Day 40----you are not going to believe this. It stopped raining. Hallelujah! Thank you Lord. Sorry for all my complaining, I knew it would stop when you said. I trusted you the whole time.

As the days went by, Noah floated patiently and waited to see dry land. However (and this is a big however) when Noah sent the dove out for the third time to see if the water had receded, the dove didn't come back. Excellent! Because this was an indication that the water was receding and there was dry land. HOWEVER, the land was not dry enough to get out of the Ark and walk on. See how smart God is. Remember back in verse 7:16 ...*then the Lord shut him in.* It was still not time for Noah to come out of the Ark although everything looked good. Noah had to wait some more. Can you imagine? I bet you can. There are some of you that have been patient and waited God's timing. And then there are those of you who got impatient and because you thought everything looked good, you got out of your Ark without God telling you to. Result; you sank! Why? Because you stepped on land that was not stable enough to hold you. Hmmm, how many times has that happened?

Noah ended up spending an entire year inside that boat before God let him out. Actually, most of the year was spent waiting patiently on dry ground than waiting for the rain to stop. God's timing was perfect!

Noah, being the obedient servant he was, waited for the Lord to unlock the door and in chapter 8:15-16:

> *"Then God says to Noah, 'Come out of the ark, you and your wife and your sons and their wives.'"*

> *"Then God blessed Noah and his sons, saying to them 'Be fruitful and increase in number and fill the earth'"* (Genesis 9:1).

> *"Everything that lives and moves will be food for you. Just as I gave you the green plants, I now give you everything"* (Genesis 9:3).

God established a covenant to never again send a flood to destroy the earth.

My friends, think about these stories the next time you are in God's "waiting room." Trust in His promises that He will increase your strength, give you rest, and you will see His goodness.

Warrior Weapon

Wait for God's Perfect Timing!

Preparing for Battle
ఈఈఈ

Read the following Scriptures:
Psalms 31:24, Psalms 62:1-6

Read the following parable: Matthew 25:1-13

What does this parable tell you about waiting?

_____

_____

_____

If we really examine ourselves, we might find that we are not waiting on God, but on someone or something else. Maybe we are waiting for our circumstances to line up just right. Whom or what are you waiting for?

_____

_____

_____

Are you putting the right things into your heart, and mind while you are waiting? What verse(s) will you specifically focus on?

_____

_____

_____

Are you waiting in a way that you will be prepared when the wait is over?

_____

_____

_____

What will you do to get prepared for when the wait is over? What specifically will you do to get prepared?

_____

_____

_____

Weapons of Truth

Memorize:

"But those who wait on the LORD

Shall renew their strength;

They shall mount up with wings like eagles,

They shall run and not be weary,

They shall walk and not faint" *(Isaiah 40:31 NKJV).*

Actions

If you haven't started a journal yet, now would be the time. I am hoping you are spending time in your Praise Journal. However, in another journal, or notebook, write down some possibilities:

The thoughts you have while in God's "waiting room."

Scriptures to encourage you during this time.

Pay attention to how God is working in your life and around you daily.

Look back on your life and see how God's timing was perfect for you.

What will you do to remain in His strength?

Digging Deeper

Spiders are very devoted creatures. Have you ever watched a spider spin a web? It's fascinating. The spider will spend many hours, sometimes days, in great effort spinning a web. As the spider spins the web, the key factor will become patience. Many hours after the web is completed, the spider waits and waits. The spider must be very still and quiet. The spider has a plan, but the plan can never develop without patience. As the spider waits, one day the spider will feel the web moving, the food has come suddenly. But there was nothing sudden about it. It was patience released (from www. Sermoncentral.com).

Don't you think our relationship with Christ prepares us for situations where we will have no other recourse but to wait? Like the spider investing time and energy into spinning its web, we must invest time and energy in getting to know Jesus. As we are still and quiet in the presence of God, His Spirit shapes our Spirit and we grow to be more like Him.

We can learn a lot from the patience of a spider. Spiders don't manipulate little bugs to crawl into their web, they simply wait. In waiting, their desires are fulfilled. As we devote ourselves to waiting on God we discover that He rewards our patience. At first glance, the reward may not look like you thought, but it will be what's best for you. God doesn't waste time. You will see His goodness and grace while in the waiting room, maybe more so then when not. Like going on vacation, sometimes the journey is more fun than the destination. What He wants us to learn is to take joy in Him no matter what. We don't exist to get what we want; we exist to bring glory to God. God's presence with us through our waiting is the reward.

How can you be more like the spider in this story?

_____

_____

_____

When was the last time you were in God's waiting room?

_____

_____

_____

How long were you there?

_____

_____

_____

What did you learn?

_____

_____

_____

If you are in His waiting room now, what are you learning?

_____

_____

_____

Find three scriptures you could use to support *The Spider*.

_____

_____

_____

Further Reading:

Waiting on God by Andrew Murray

Chapter 7
❧❧❧

Matters of the Heart

"Above all else, guard our heart, for it is the wellspring of life"
(Proverbs 4:23).

What's in Your Heart?

When my friend's young son was in a pre-kindergarten class he was caught one day dripping wet after putting his head in the toilet. The teacher asked Billy, "Why did you stick your head in the toilet?" Billy replied, "I don't know, but I didn't drink any."

I have those days also. Not that I stick my head in the toilet, but I wonder why I did something I didn't really want to do but did it anyway, worse yet, I then try to twist the story so it doesn't look as bad as it really is. Here is Billy's story, minus the toilet.

"So the trouble is not with the law, for it is spiritual and good. The trouble is with me, for I am all too human, a slave to sin. 15I don't really understand myself, for I want to do what is right, but I don't do it. Instead, I do what I hate. 16But if I know that what I am doing is wrong, this shows that I agree that the law is good. 17So I am not the one doing

wrong; it is sin living in me that does it. ¹⁸"And I know that nothing good lives in me, that is, in my sinful nature, I want to do what is right, but I can't. ¹⁹I want to do what is good, but I don't. I don't want to do what is wrong, but I do it anyway. ²⁰But if I do what I don't want to do, I am not really the one doing wrong; it is sin living in me that does it. ²¹"I have discovered this principle of life—that when I want to do what is right, I inevitably do what is wrong. ²²I love God's law with all my heart. ²³But there is another power within me that is at war with my mind. This power makes me a slave to the sin that is still within me. ²⁴Oh, what a miserable person I am! Who will free me from this life that is dominated by sin and death? ²⁵Thank God! The answer is in Jesus Christ our Lord. So you see how it is: In my mind I really want to obey God's law, but because of my sinful nature I am a slave to sin" (Romans 7:14-25 NLT).

I think we all can relate to these words written by the Apostle Paul. Many times I say the same thing he does in verse 15:

"I don't really understand myself, for I want to do what is right, but I don't do it. Instead, I do what I hate."

Now the excuse comes in verse 17:

"So I am not the one doing wrong; it is sin living in me that does it."

In other words, "The Devil made me do it."

Now this is true, we are born sinners, and we shouldn't underestimate the power of our enemy, as we discussed in Chapter 3. However, we are still responsible for our actions and choices. The problem is, we keep forgetting we are fighting a defeated enemy.

To gain some clarity on what Paul was trying to tell us, let's look at the following illustration.

We belong to a team called the "Angels." We are in the Championship game and our opponent is the "Boo Devils." We play the game, Jesus, our star player, takes us to victory. We Win! Game Over!

Then the next day, the "Boo Devils" come to us and demand a rematch. They want to play the Championship game again. We, the "Angels," instead of declining, refusing to answer, walking away, or repeating how we have claimed victory, we choose to fight the battle again. In other words, we decide to play again a game we have already played and won.

The truth is all we had to do was look at our star player, "Excuse me, already won this battle, game over." However, the powerhouse of the "Boo Devils" doesn't like being defeated so he uses his craftiness and poisonous charm to convince the "Angels" to agree with him, not to trust the win, and to play again. The fleshy "Angels" fall for his schemes and give in to another competition with the "Boo Devils."

This story illustrates the battle of our old nature against our new nature. This battle comes from within our heart.

Once we accept Christ as our Savior, we have a new heart. And as Romans 8:1 promises,

> *"Therefore, there is now no condemnation to them that are in Christ Jesus."*

So, here we are on the Championship team, new hearts and everything, but our opponent keeps shooting accusations at our team, with the target being our heart, hoping we'll give in and keep playing the game until he wins.

> *So, it becomes the devil's business to keep the Christian's spirit imprisoned."* A.W. Tozer

This reminds me of a popular commercial promoting a credit card company. This company claims the carrying of their card will bring protection, comfort and the peace of mind. The intriguing question they ask is, "What's in your wallet?"

A similar question should be proposed to us as team "Angels." Instead of "What's in your wallet," our question is, "What's in your heart?" This, my friend, is where it all starts.

If God were to look into your heart, what would He find?

Anger, Guilt, Bitterness, Pride, Emptiness, Loneliness, Pain.

This isn't about religion or rules or ways to behave. It's not about doing the right thing, going to church, or a Bible study, drinking or not, going to R-rated movies, this or that. It is about what is going on in your heart. Jesus isn't into healing the symptoms. He wants to heal your heart!

As Broken Warriors, let the healing begin! I know I am excited about the transformation. We can stop lying to ourselves and to God. We can seek Him with all our heart, confess to Him all that is in our heart, and the Lord will bring us back from captivity. Hallelujah!

> [11] *"For I know the plans I have for you," declares the LORD, "plans to prosper you and not to harm you, plans to give you hope and a future. [12] Then you will call upon me and come and pray to me, and I will listen to you. [13] You will seek me and find me when you seek me with all your heart. [14] I will be found by you," declares the LORD, "and will bring you back from captivity. [a] I will gather you from all*

the nations and places where I have banished you," declares
the LORD, "and will bring you back to the place from which
I carried you into exile" (Jeremiah 29:11-14).

Heart Transplant

Spend some time on the question, "What's in your heart?"
After this process, you might conclude you need a new heart. God,
our Great Physician, did a heart transplant for the Israelites.

> *25 "I will sprinkle clean water on you, and you will be clean;*
> *I will cleanse you from all your impurities and from all*
> *your idols. 26 I will give you a new heart and put a new*
> *spirit in you; I will remove from you your heart of stone*
> *and give you a heart of flesh. 27 And I will put my Spirit in*
> *you and move you to follow my decrees and be careful to*
> *keep my laws"* (Ezekiel 36:25-27).

To help you understand the concept, the verse before this
passage describes how God sent the people of Israel into exile
because of their disobedience and out-right defiance. They were not
honoring His holy name; they were defying the land, worshipping
idols, etc.

God, however, promised He wouldn't leave them forever
and even though they didn't deserve the land He had promised, He
brought them back—restored. The process involved removing their

hearts of stone, and giving them new hearts, soft, pliable, trusting, and "open to change" hearts. God also gave them His Spirit to help them transform.

The questions we need to ask ourselves are:

*Are we as open to God as we should be?

*Is our heart soft and willing to love and trust?

*Do we need a heart transplant?

These questions require us to go deeper. It is like having "soul surgery." It is scary to go into surgery of any kind. Let's say during our exploratory surgery, we discover we need a heart transplant. Instead of getting a new heart, we just keep trying to patch up our old heart. Maybe this is why we can't move forward. We are too busy repairing holes, stitching up seams, finding new ways to hold this old heart together. Why won't we accept the new heart we have been given? Sound familiar? This is replaying the game, a game in which we have already claimed victory.

Our hearts can be deceptive, easily convincing us we want what someone else has. Our hearts are emotional, prone to wander spiritually. God has promised if we give control of our hearts to Him, we will be transformed from the inside out!

Jesus uses an illustration in Matthew 9:16 to remind us He came to bring wholeness, not to patch us up only to fall apart again.

"No one sews a patch of unshrunk cloth on an old garment, for the patch will pull away from the garment, making the tear worse."

The point is, we have a new life and can choose to accept this new heart every day. God doesn't intend for us to worry about the scars of the old heart; God never meant for circumstances to drive our lives. He came to give us new life. Accept and receive the new heart and stop trying to *revive* the old one.

No matter how destructive the habit, thoughts, or relationship, God can transform. When you seek Him, ask Him for this new heart. Ask Him to extract the stony heart. Extract the traumatized heart, which carries so much pain. Maybe what needs removing is the heart that won't let you get close to anyone. Ask our Healer to remove the cold-hardened heart and give you a warm, soft heart that is open to Him.

Warrior Weapon

I will examine my heart and give control of my heart to Jesus.

Guard your Heart

This new improved heart doesn't come with a lot of instructions, but there are a couple of things we should know.

To get to know our own hearts, and to help us to have an obedient heart, God has given us the Spirit to teach us, which also means spending time in His Word.

> *"But the Counselor, the Holy Spirit, whom the Father will send in my name, will teach you all things and will remind you of everything I have said to you"* (John 14:26).

Understand it is easy for us to sin. Why, Because...

> *"The heart is deceitful above all things and beyond cure. Who can understand it? "I the LORD search the heart and examine the mind, to reward a man according to his conduct, according to what his deeds deserve"* (Jeremiah 17:9-10).

Guard your heart.

> *"Above all else, guard your heart, for it is the wellspring of life"* (Proverbs 4:23).

Note this last verse says, "Above all else." Solomon, the author of Proverbs, makes this very clear as he emphasizes the importance of the following act of guarding your heart by a demand of "Above *all* else." Why, because the heart is the wellspring of life. Solomon used wellspring as an illustration as to the importance of the heart. The issues of life come out of the heart and the heart is our continuous source of supply. Our hearts are the source of everything we say and do. The heart carries our desires, hopes, dreams, affections, motivations-what we care most about. So even a little sin in our wellspring has the power to pollute and corrupt the very essence of who we are. Now you see why it is important as to what goes in the heart, for it is the wellspring of life. Hence the command, "Above all else, guard."

I find it ironic King Solomon wrote this wise proverb at the beginning of his reign. Towards the end of his reign look what happens:

> *"The Lord became angry with Solomon because his heart had turned away from the Lord, the God of Israel, who had appeared to him twice. Although he had forbidden Solomon to follow other gods, Solomon did not keep the Lord's command. So the Lord said to Solomon, 'Since this is your attitude and you have not keep my covenant and my decrees, which I commanded you, I will most certainly tear the kingdom away from you and give it to one of your subordinates'"* (1 Kings 11:9-12).

Solomon started out as the wisest man ever lived, but he ended his life in disgrace and ruin because he didn't guard his heart. He began compromising God's principles.

I think we are capable of doing the same thing. We start mixing and mingling the holy with the unholy. I have heard it said the most miserable people on earth are those who struggle with one foot in the kingdom and one foot in this world.

In a nighttime drama series on TV, a woman who is married to a prominent man, tries to guard her heart. Her husband has had public affairs and legal issues. At her place of employment, a gentleman friend is trying to take care of her by saying all the right things, being kind and showing her respect. He starts calling her at home at night. At first, it's innocent and only about work. Then they start meeting about work projects after hours. She feels an attraction to this man. Her heart is empty. He is no doubt attracted to her. His affections toward her are becoming obvious and she is battling her feelings towards him and is trying to avoid him. One particular evening he calls, she doesn't answer because she knows she might fall in the "moment of the maybe." He leaves a message on her cell and she listens intently. As she listens, her heart begins to race. His words start to fill an empty heart. However, as she realizes the poison of these words, and who they are coming from, she hangs up. In essence, she was protecting her wellspring.

Our empty heart sounds a trumpet to the enemy and he flies in with his disguises and deceptions. Have you ever noticed when you have those thoughts, feelings of discouragement, loneliness, or other feelings of despair, a bag of Oreos looks like the perfect answer? Maybe the answer the enemy has proposed to you is drugs, alcohol, the arms of another, lies, or even gossip. Many things appeal to an empty heart. When your heart is full, and these proposed answers come up, the heart doesn't give in. Jesus reminds us:

> *"The thief comes only to steal and kill and destroy; I have come that they may have life, and have it to the full"*
> (John 10:10).

Warrior Weapon

Keep my heart full of His truth! I will Guard my Heart!

Guard Essentials

Are you keeping your heart full? Are you aware of the enemy and his deceptive ways? Are you on guard for your heart? These are the questions we have proposed so far. What are some more things we can do to guard our hearts? Consider:

1. How are you spending your time? Is what you are reading, or watching filling your heart with thoughts of God?

2. Do you know what God's thoughts even are? You can know by spending time with Him daily and filling your mind with His ways. His filling is not just water, but

Living Water (John 4:10-14). Knowing the Truth will set you free.

3. Choose obedience to His Word.
    a. Listening to God requires discipline and self-restraint to ignore all the other messages filtering in about what or where you should be in life. The irony is, God's messages are as clear as the ungodly messages. We have only to stop and listen to hear His voice.

4. Watch where you go, who your friends are, what you set your affections on. Maybe you need to let go of some things, or someone.

Letting Go

All his young life, this little boy wanted to see an eagle fly. He had heard so much about them in school but this trip would give him the opportunity to see an eagle. Every day he went out to the field with his binoculars hoping to catch a glance of this spectacular bird. Then one evening it happened, he looked up and saw this monstrous sight flying through the air. Soaring at a great height, the eagle's wing span must have been eight to nine feet.

The character of an eagle is something to admire. The eagle uses what he has, and he does what he is created for, soaring. He has incredible abilities and uses them wisely. He even knows to use his abilities to push him higher so when storms come, he is not in the midst of them, but soars above them. He even mates for life. Much can be learned from the eagle.

As the boy watched the eagle fly, he saw him suddenly shoot to the ground like a torpedo, snatch something from the ground, and then shoot back up into the sky. As the eagle climbed higher, in mid-air, he then came to a sudden stop. His next move was not graceful or magnificent; you see, the eagle started plummeting to the ground. He was falling, as if he had been shot. But no gunshot was heard by the boy. As the boy looked on, the bird flapped and fell to the earth. The boy, confused and scared, ran to the majestic bird only to find him face down in the dirt, not moving. The majestic eagle, who just minutes ago was soaring, was dead. The boy was crying and cautiously rolled the eagle over and there, affixed to the great bird's chest, was a weasel—one of the lowliest of common ground critters. This ordinary weasel had bitten through the regal chest, into the heart of the eagle. (Story adapted from T.D. Jakes)

What happened? The eagle picked up something that he wouldn't let go. He was stronger than the weasel, and the weasel couldn't have hurt him, unless he picked him up. However, because the eagle did not let go of the weasel, he could not guard his heart. The very thing the eagle held on to killed him.

What are you holding onto? What is holding you? What is biting at your heart? Is it what your eyes are seeing? What your ears are hearing? The heart determines our behavior. Be careful, it doesn't always happen in a day, it's a slow fade.

Warrior Weapon

Determine what is killing my heart, polluting my wellspring and then LET IT GO!

My sweet friends, our hearts do matter to God, so much so that He paid a tremendous price. "*For God so loved the world that he gave his one and only son*" (John 3:16). Shouldn't we care about our hearts? What will you do about your wellspring? Let's start filling our wellspring right now with some of His truths, promises, and Living Water.

" *Create in me a pure heart, O God,*
and renew a steadfast spirit within me" (Psalm 51:10).

"*Delight yourself in the LORD*
and he will give you the desires of your heart" (Psalm 37:4).

"*Blessed are they who keep his statutes*
and seek him with all their heart" (Psalm 119:2).

*"As water reflects a face,
so a man's heart reflects the man"* (Proverbs 27:19).

"Blessed are the pure in heart, for they will see God"
(Matthew 5:8).

*"O Jerusalem, wash the evil from your heart and be saved.
How long will you harbor wicked thoughts"* (Jeremiah
4:14)?

*"I will give them a heart to know me, that I am the LORD.
They will be my people, and I will be their God, for they will
return to me with all their heart"* (Jeremiah 24:7).

*He said to them, "You are the ones who justify yourselves in
the eyes of men, but God knows your hearts. What is highly
valued among men is detestable in God's sight"* (Luke 16:15).

*"One of those listening was a woman named Lydia, a dealer
in purple cloth from the city of Thyatira, who was a
worshiper of God. The Lord opened her heart to respond to
Paul's message"* (Acts 16:14).

*"Therefore, judge nothing before the appointed time; wait
till the Lord comes. He will bring to light what is hidden in
darkness and will expose the motives of men's hearts. At*

that time each will receive his praise from God"
*(*1 Corinthians 4:5).

"Since, then, you have been raised with Christ, set your hearts on things above, where Christ is seated at the right hand of God" (Colossians 3:1).

"Let the peace of Christ rule in your hearts, since as members of one body you were called to peace. And be thankful" (Colossians 3:15).

"Here I am! I stand at the door and knock. If anyone hears my voice and opens the door, I will come in and eat with him, and he with me" (Revelation 3:20).

As Broken Warriors, let's leave the doors of our hearts open to God. He is our only hope for lasting fulfillment!

Preparing for Battle
ക്-ക്-ക്

What are you doing in your life that you know is wrong, but want to do right? Why do you think you keep making this choice?

_____

_____

_____

What will you do today, tomorrow, and the next day to stop this wrong choice? Write down your plan of action.

_____

_____

_____

How would you answer the question: "What's in your heart?"

_____

_____

_____

What are you doing that is polluting your wellspring?

_____

_____

_____

How will you guard your heart daily? Write down your plan of action.

_____

_____

_____

Action

Look up and rewrite the verses listed on the previous page in a different translation. The translation used was the New International Version.

Which of those "Weapons of Truth" will you choose to memorize?

Weapons of Truth

Memorize:

"Above all else, guard your heart, for it is the wellspring of life" (Proverbs 4:23).

Digging Deeper

Read 1 Kings 10 and 11.

How was Solomon compromising God's principles?

_____

_____

_____

Chapter 8
Җ҉ Җ҉ Җ҉

Bringing in the Sheeps

"...he restoreth my soul" (Psalm 23:3 KJV).

As a little girl, I remember sitting on a hard wooden pew about five rows from the back of the church. A man standing at the front of the church announced our next hymn. This was always my favorite part of the service. He would say, "Turn to page 196 in your hymnals and stand with me while we sing "Bringing in the Sheaves." Ok, I have to admit, even though I could read the words in the hymnal, I always thought they were singing "Bringing in the Sheeps." When we would sing the line, "We will come rejoicing bringing in the sheeps," I just thought they had lost their sheep and now they were happy to find them all. What's a sheave anyway?

I don't think this song is even listed in hymnals anymore. This hymn, written in the late 1800s, was inspired from Psalm 126. The bottom line: the subject of Psalm 126 is Restoration.

My friends, God is in the Restoration business. As Broken Warriors, expect to need restoration, even in those times when your faith appears to be flourishing.

When God renews us, He restores us; or when He restores us, we are renewed. Either way, there are numerous stories in the Bible of God's restoring not only people but also nations. I'm sure there are many of you who could tell your own story of renewal and how God brought you back to Him. What seems to be a common thread of restoration throughout many of the stories in the Bible is bringing His people back from the state of loneliness.

Do you have a heart haunted by loneliness? Do you have a cry inside your soul no one sees or knows about? God feels our pain and comforts us when our journey is a lonely one. He does understand the pain we suffer. God will comfort us, and will make good out of what was intended for evil.

I pray the following words will bring encouragement to you as we soak up His Word, His thoughts, and His ways.

Lonely Days, Lonely Nights

Did you know that one of the most growing problems in our society is loneliness? Think about it, because of our technology and thrust to get more, our loneliness-producing society discourages intimacy and actually stimulates loneliness. We can run a thriving business from any room in our house, and never actually see anyone.

Loneliness affects all ages, not just the elderly widow, or widowers, as most think. Divorced people and single parents are typically the next on our list. However, you might be surprised to find out that a study by the American Council of Life Insurance reported that the age group who feels the loneliest most often are college students.

Many factors can cause these feelings of loneliness. You might be surprised to learn the most common cause of loneliness is guilt. Rejection and abandonment by others rank high as well. A few other factors are fear and insecurities, role changes, such as your role of being a full-time mom (kids grow up and move away), or retirement. Some of you may be feeling lonely because you have made spiritual decisions that separate you from your family. Also, don't get hung up on loneliness meaning being alone. I have been in a room full of family and friends, and have felt like the loneliest soul in existence. And I know some of you know exactly what I mean.

Understand also, we are not talking about solitude. Solitude is a voluntary withdrawal from people.

Have you ever felt lonely and thought, "Maybe if I will just surround myself with a lot of people, I won't feel so lonely?" During our struggles of infertility, the years of being childless were sometimes unbearable. Even though happily married, the waves of loneliness were drowning my heart. I would go to the mall thinking shopping might take my mind off those feelings, only to end up feeling lonelier than ever. I saw others pushing strollers and holding hands with their children. Because of this intense loneliness I had, my lens on life was skewed. Everything I wanted, (a child), but didn't have was being magnified. There could have been a family of skunks walking around in the mall and all I would see is how they were a "perfect little family." Crazy I know, but true.

I was letting my lonely feelings control my life. Loneliness became my stronghold. Now don't get me wrong - these feelings are real, and sometimes justified. But like strongholds, I had let something that should be temporary become controlling. In the following verse, the psalmist feels lonely and depressed but chooses to remember that the living God is His Savior.

"Why are you downcast, O my soul?
Why so disturbed within me?
Put your hope in God,
for I will yet praise him,
my Savior" (Psalm 42:5).

Lonely Warriors

Mother Teresa expressed feelings of loneliness in a letter she wrote. "I am told God lives in me, and yet the reality of darkness and coldness and emptiness is so great that nothing touches my soul." My fellow Broken Warrior, you are not alone. Even those who have been such an ambassador for His Kingdom have those feelings of despair.

When I think of Corrie Ten Boom and the feelings of loneliness she must have felt, my heart aches. The Nazi guards captured Corrie for helping hide the Jews from the concentration camps. Here she was, a woman who had spent the last fifty-two years surrounded by her loving family, and suddenly she was utterly alone. She was captured and in solitary confinement. Her cell was only a few paces wide. She described standing with her back to the wall, spreading out her hands, and pressing against the sides—as if she were trying to hold them from closing in on her. Can you even imagine? There was no one to talk to and she wasn't allowed to sing hymns to herself. Corrie Ten Boom was restored! She lived to carry her message of triumph through God's strength to people all over the world.

What about the woman in Luke 8:43-48? Her name was not listed, she is known only as "woman." This woman had a bleeding disorder for twelve years. Because of her bleeding, she was considered unclean, untouchable, an outcast. She couldn't even go to the temple to worship the Lord. Imagine the despair she had, the extreme feelings of aloneness. I imagine the stares and whispers of others only worsened her feelings.

This woman heard stories about the Nazarene teacher named Jesus. How did she hear about this prophet? Even though she walked alone, she still heard the stories. God made sure of it. She heard about His miracles, His healings. She thought, "Maybe He, this healer, could touch me and heal me." Or maybe, I could just touch Him, even just touch His cloak." But wait, she was unclean, He wouldn't want to touch her. If she did manage to touch Him, that would make Him unclean. The crowd would most definitely stone her for making the Teacher unclean. And how humiliating would it be if she could get to Jesus in the crowd and have to explain to Him what was wrong, why she needed healing.

It had been twelve years of seeing doctors, trying different remedies, twelve years of physical and emotional pain. She was desperate. She was depressed, frail, weak, and extremely lonely.

What gave her strength to get there? What gave her strength and courage to get over her fear to touch him? She had *faith* that the prophet, the Teacher, the Messiah could heal her if she could just get to him.

This nameless woman makes the choice one day to put feet to her faith. As the story goes, she risked everything. She made her way through the crowd that was following Jesus, came up behind Him, and touched the edge of His cloak. Immediately, her bleeding stopped. Jesus restored her! However, not just from disease, but from the ever-debilitating feeling of loneliness. Jesus assured this restoration by having a conversation with her and renewing her to others by publicly saying with an endearing term, "Daughter, your faith has healed you. Go in peace."

Jesus, our Shepherd, restored her soul! Jesus, our Shepherd, wants to restore yours as well. Will you let Him?

Warrior Weapon

I will put feet to my faith and take steps toward restoration!

Steps of Renewal

Taking the cue from this nameless woman of Luke 8, look at some action steps for restoration from loneliness:

* Step out in faith. Put feet to your prayers.

> *"In the same way, faith by itself, if it is not accompanied by action, is dead"* (James 2:17).

* When you begin to feel any sign of loneliness, let's view that as a call from God to spend some time with Him. He isn't causing your loneliness or ignoring it either. He just wants to be the One who fills the empty spaces.

> *"...To those who have been called, who are loved by God the Father and kept by Jesus Christ: Mercy, peace and love be yours in abundance"* (Jude 1:1-2).

> *"Loneliness is an opportunity for Jesus to make Himself known."* F.B Meyer

*We are the ones who decide how we will let loneliness affect us. Will we choose intimacy with Christ, or relief which the shallow, temporary world offers? Bill Gothard makes a great point when he says "Loneliness becomes our 'friend' when it forces us to enjoy the friendship of God as much as we would   the friendship of others."

> "*For the wisdom of this world is foolishness in God's sight...*" (1 Corinthians 3:19).

* Is your loneliness caused by you expecting others to meet your needs as only God can?

> "*Find rest, O my soul, in God alone; my hope comes from him*" (Psalm 62:5).

* When King David was facing problems of loneliness, he would find his strength and solutions in the Lord.

> "*David was greatly distressed because the men were talking of stoning him; each one was bitter I spirit because of his sons and daughters. But David found strength in the Lord his God*" (1 Samuel 30:6).

*Know when you are lonely you are at risk- risk of being tempted, distracted, and seduced. Extended times in God's presence will deepen your roots and strengthen your soul.

"Come, let us bow down in worship, let us kneel before the Lord our Maker" (Psalm 95:6).

*Praying is the most important way to deal with loneliness, and fellowship comes next.

"Let us not give up meeting together, as some are in the habit of doing, but let us encourage one another—and all the more as you see the Day approaching" (Hebrews 10:25).

*Serve others.

"You, my brothers, were called to be free. But do not use your freedom to indulge the sinful nature; rather, serve one another in love" (Galatians 5:13).

*Memorize Scripture:

Purchase a two-ring index cardholder and write down some of your favorite scriptures. Use your time waiting at the doctor's office or in the carpool lane to memorize His promises and truths. Here are some scriptures to get you started:

Psalm 46:1, Isaiah 41:10, Matthew 28:20, Hebrews 13:5

*Write a list of your thoughts that cause you to feel lonely.

*Then next to that statement—rewrite it with an opposite statement.

For example; "When surrounded by people, I know no one wants me around them."

Re-write as realistic. "Someone in this room feels like I do. I can encourage someone here."

Most of our thoughts are usually false beliefs, which keep us in bondage to loneliness or other feelings of despair. Take these statements of loneliness and turn them into a prayer to God. Taking the first example you might say something like:

> *Father, I feel so lonely even when I am around a lot of people. I don't want to feel this way. Being around others just seems to magnify my hurt. Give me courage and strength to be around others and make friends and know others may feel the same way I do. Let me be an encouragement to them.*

*Choose to live Loved! Choose to believe God loves you, and receive His love. He will give your life significance. When we accept God's evaluation of us, we won't be controlled by our own feelings of inadequacy and loneliness. When we live with His confidence, we can be all He created us to be. He gives us purpose! When you know you are loved, it changes the way you feel about yourself. Pray for God to help you accept His love. God will not refuse to answer that prayer.

"We love because he first loved us" (1 John 4:19).

*A powerful thought hit me between the eyes when I read Psalm 37:4: "Delight yourself in the Lord and he will give you the desires of your heart." It made me stop and think: "When I am feeling lonely, does God feel the same loneliness towards me because my basic delight is not in Him?"

> *"When you are lonely too much stillness is exactly the thing that seems to be laying waste your soul, but use that stillness to quiet your heart before God. Get to know Him."* Elisabeth Elliott

*Know that we may be alone, but we don't have to be lonely all the time. Jesus experienced a horrific death for us so we could have the love, presence, fellowship, and guidance of God forever.

> *"Yet I am always with you;*
> *you hold me by my right hand.*
> *You guide me with your counsel,*
> *and afterward you will take me into glory.*
> *Whom have I in heaven but you?"*

> *"And earth has nothing I desire besides you.*
> *My flesh and my heart may fail,*

but God is the strength of my heart
and my portion forever ..."

"As for me, it is good to be near God.
I have made the Sovereign LORD my refuge;
I will tell of all your deeds" (Psalm 76:23-26, 28).

Warrior Weapon

Renewal is something a Broken Warrior should strive for.

Restoration

In my senior year of high school, I worked and saved my money to buy a used sports car. To be exact, it was a coffee brown, 1976, Datsun 280Z. After several years of being exposed to Missouri's weather of snow and ice, combined with the poor mechanical , the car was what you would call "rusted out." In 1985, a friend said he would help us restore the car. As I drove, I could see the road through a hole in the floorboard. For sure, I knew the time had come as when I drove in the rain and hit a water puddle. The water would shoot up through the floor and drench my shoes and pants. This was never a funny thing.

It took several months to restore this car, but it was worth it. We took an old rusted out car, restored it, and painted it a confident red. It looked brand new. I didn't care how many water puddles I went through now.

The basic concept of restoration is to turn back, make "whole" again, to be complete. This is exactly what God does to us. He makes us "whole;" He completes us. However, God restores us from the inside out.

You might think that while being in the Good Shepherd's care you would never become so distressed your soul would need restoration, but it does happen, because we are human

Numerous stories of restoration are in the Bible. David, Elijah, Moses, Jeremiah, Peter, Rahab, -these are a small sampling of the people God restored. Don't forget God restored nations, as well.   In 2 Chronicles 7:13-15, it is God's plan to restore Israel. Verse 14 sums it up:

> *"Then if my people who are called by my name, will humble themselves and pray and seek my face and turn from their wicked ways, then I will hear from heaven and will forgive their sin and restore their land."*

Notice the action words in this verse, then the reward.

Action words:
Humble-Pray-Turn-Seek
Reward:
Restore (heal) (reconcile) (renew)

What a great list of principles and steps to restoration. Take the above verse and take it as your own. For Example: *"Then if you (your name)_____will humble yourself and pray and seek my face and turn from your wicked ways, then I will hear you and forgive your sins and will restore you."*

Rejoicing Restoration

In the book of Zephaniah, God uses this prophet to shake the people of Judah out of their complacency, urging them to return to God. In other words, he tells them: "Stop sinning, stop doing your own thing in your own way, and repent. God will restore your land and your relationship with Him.

Only three chapters long, Zephaniah describes the sin of people who have turned away from God, who choose to live according to their own rules. There was disobedience, and of course poor choices because of lack of obedience, which led to some bad consequences. Ever had that happen? I cannot tell you the number of times this has happened to me. I ran into many walls before I finally had sense enough to stop. Unfortunately, it finally took an accident to make me still enough to get what I call a "good talkin' to" from the Lord. However, he restored me. I was like the people of Judah. I wouldn't have classified it as turning away from God, that sounds so harsh, but in essence, that is what I did, and often do. Yikes! See what I mean by *daily* restoration.

As you continue reading in Zephaniah, you will see correction followed sin. Correction is usually followed by repentance - turning back to God and away from sin. Repentance also brings about the restoration of the relationship between God and us. Hmm, does this pattern of principles look familiar? Even when we sin, God loves us with all His heart. Nothing changes God's love for us. (Sounds like something to thank Him for in our journal). Praise Him for His love endures forever - no matter what!

Zephaniah continues to explain that God, OUR God, stays in the midst of our lives. His presence is real. God is fighting, not against us, but for us (Romans 8:31). God is working in our lives to bring us to the point of reconciliation and restoration when we sin. Thank you Lord!

I have a plaque on my wall that reads:

"The Lord your God is with you, he is mighty to save. He will take great delight in you, he will quiet you with his love; he will rejoice over you with singing" (Zephaniah 3:17).

When was the last time you rejoiced over someone with singing because you loved him or her so much? If you are honest and lucky, you might have in the early stages of children or marriage. But, is this something you do daily? God does with us.

Now, you just might be saying to yourself, "What, really? You mean God loves me even after I behaved like I did and said those awful words to my family?" Yes. "God loves me even after I have looked for everything else to fill my empty heart except for Him?" Yes!

Look at how the Lord reacts to children who turn to Him:

*Rejoices over us with gladness, takes delight in us
*Renews us with love, quiets the turmoil in our lives with love
*Rejoices over us with singing

These phrases describe a God who is joyful, excited, and full of love. This is how God sees you, Broken Warrior, and desires that you want to turn to Him.

I could list many more scriptures about His restoration, but I think what God wants me to share with you more than the "big stuff." Not how He can take a marriage in shambles and renew it; not how you can be near death and be restored by His hand; not how He can bring the prodigal child home—not just the big stuff, but the everyday experiences, as well. God wants' us to know He can (and will) restore us daily. He desires to restore us day by day. You don't think you need moment by moment restoration? You want to wait for the "big stuff?" I am learning how quickly my selfishness distorts my relationship with Him and how badly I need that instant renewal, rejuvenation, and restoration. I need reconciliation daily!

The Lord wants is to be our life, not just *part* of our life. God tells us He loves us. He showed us He loves us by the most sacrificial act known to humanity. Shouldn't that be enough*? I ask myself all the time, how much more proof do you need, Tanya*? It is a hard idea to wrap your mind and heart around knowing the Lord loves us unconditionally. As much as my parents loved me, I still have never been loved the way Jesus loves me, and neither have you. As much as we love our family and friends, we are not capable of loving unconditionally. But God is, and does! As Broken Warriors, let us help each other accept God's great love for us.

Warrior Weapon

I will rejoice in God's restoration!

Casted Sheep

During the writing process of this study, I sat at my computer hour after hour. As a result, I began to experience much pain, and cramps in my lower legs and feet. These cramps kept me up at night. There were some mornings I looked pretty funny hobbling around as I tried to straighten my legs out. At this point, I began to think of myself as a "casted" sheep. This is the term used for a sheep that has turned over on its back and can't get back up.

This is a very pathetic sight. The sheep is frightened, frustrated, and frantic—trying to right itself, but without success. If the sheep does not get help quickly, he could die.

Then I began to think of the importance and responsibility of a shepherd. The Shepherd watches over his flock daily. Knowing the whereabouts of each and every sheep. When one is missing, the shepherd starts his search. Many times, he finds the panic-stricken sheep in need of rescue.

After the long sessions of writing, I identified greatly with this sheep. In the daytime, I wrote and many times rejoiced at the insights God gave me for you. I could hardly contain my excitement (just like free-romping sheep), but at night the cramps came and I was vulnerable to discouragement and doubt, and became frightened and frustrated...just like the casted sheep.

The inexperienced shepherd who finds the sheep on its back has the immediate impulse of picking it up and carrying it. The seasoned shepherd, however, knows that could cause death. The experience shepherd rolls the sheep on its side to relieve the gas in the rumen; massages the limbs to restore circulation; holds the sheep up while straddling it between his legs, and constantly reassures the sheep of his presence and care. Set free from its fears, the sheep regains its strength and balance, rejoining the flock. Renewed and Restored!

This is what our Good Shepherd does for us as "casted"

sheep. He watches over us daily, coming after us when we wander. He hears our cries. He restores us when we are flat on our backs with no vision of being upright again. His renewing and restoring love gives us strength to rejoin the flock...*he restoreth my soul!*

> *"God uses broken things. It takes broken soil to produce a crop, broken clouds to give rain, broken grain to give bread, broken bread to give strength. It is the broken alabaster box that gives forth perfume. It is Peter, weeping bitterly, who returns to greater power than ever."* Vance Havner

Unfortunately, my friends, our journey together has ended. I enjoyed envisioning each of your faces, with God being with you every word you read. I wish I could talk to each one of you about your own personal journey.

My mission for writing this study was to share insights with you to guide you through everyday life, the insights that God graciously shared with me. Whether you have walked closely with the Lord for many years or a friend dragged you into this study, I pray you are on your way to becoming renewed, and restored.

At what point in our journey did you realize you were a Broken Warrior? Was it before you picked up the book? I am wondering if your first thoughts when you read or heard the title, *Broken Warrior*, were, "Oh, that's me." I am hoping now as we have walked together these last few weeks, you get the punch line: being a Broken Warrior, is a good thing! Your brokenness has brought you to a place of intimacy with God. Your brokenness strengthens you, and gives you the ability (much like the eagle) to soar... soar high above every circumstance of life.

I am praying you have learned as much as I have during our time together. We have learned that no matter what, we are to remain in Him, because apart from Him we can do nothing! We have learned how to equip ourselves against our enemy's attacks. We will strive daily to increase our faith, and patiently wait on His guidance. We have been encouraged to let go of things that cause our hearts to hurt. Guarding our hearts will become an active role for us. We desire to clothe ourselves in humility and become mighty Praise Warriors.

Until we meet again, I will pray for your faith to be ignited, and for you to live a changed life. A life that glorifies God in all you do; A *Broken Warriors* life.

"Live Weak, Live Loved, Live Broken."